Endorsements

Women of God, you are not alone! In this book, you will find much-needed encouragement and the strength with courage to stand in FAITH during your worst season. God is near, and with certainty, He hears your cry. Laila and Elisa have beautifully woven a tapestry of hand-picked women who know God and were willing to share their "God Story" within the pages of this book. This powerful sister team continues to bring the heart of God to the soul of His daughters. If you need a "word" to carry you into tomorrow, this is it: I Cried, and He Heard Me.

--Pastor Ron Lewis
Global Apostolic Leader, Founder of Every Nation
Churches: NYC and Kings Park

You only have to meet Laila and Elisa once to encounter the passion they have for Jesus and their heart to see others know the love, joy, and peace that only He can give. It is no wonder that they felt led to put this "anthology" together. It is more than a collection of stories. It is a treasure - where women can find the eternal gems of power, courage, and hope to overcome any obstacle in their lives.

--Kathy Troccoli
Singer, Speaker, Author

It is a pleasure to write heartfelt comments about my friends Laila and Elisa. These sisters are some of the finest ladies there are. They have a tremendous love for our Lord, for people, and for life itself. After starting a successful online ministry two years ago called SorellaLIVE, Laila and Elisa now have a book called I Cried, and He Heard Me. The anthology concept is wonderful. Twenty-eight women of various backgrounds freely share meaningful testimonies about their encounters with the Lord. After being in a healing ministry for over 30 years, I have learned the importance of hearing someone's story. As these ladies share with you personal moments where they needed God to answer them, you will be moved and encouraged that God will do the same for you.

--Rev. Jim Hockaday
Jim Hockaday Ministries International

In my years of knowing Laila and Elisa, I have watched their gifts and calling develop into two powerful women of God! They both have unique anointings in which they walk in with great confidence and with an awareness of God's presence. Now, as a team, a dynamic duo, I'm blessed to see them moving in the Holy Spirit's direction with a heart for the harvest.

Two sisters united in reaching women from diverse backgrounds with God's love and compassion and inspiring them to move forward into all God has created them to be! This anointed anthology will be an inspirational resource for women all over the world in receiving hope for the hopeless and stirring faith in the hearts of the reader!

--Liliane Vernaud
Missionary in DRCongo

SorellaLIVE is encouraging women with the power of God's Word. These women know the challenges that life brings, and, more importantly, they know where we can find rest for our weary souls. No one has to fight the battle alone. SorellaLIVE is building a community where women can find hope, comfort, and healing. They are inspiring women to use their God-given gifts to invest in the people around them. This collection of powerful stories will help you meet the challenges you're facing with fresh hope and perseverance. You are not alone! As you read the stories of your fellow travelers, you will find the strength to embrace the adventure God has for you.

--Dr. Gabriel Bouch
Lead Pastor, Freedom Church

We all choose whether we will live by design or by default. Living life by design is possible. We all have a God-given destiny to fulfill while we are here on this earth, yet daily, people everywhere live in bondage and below the poverty line of their divine purpose. Challenging situations are more real now than ever, and people need to know that God will hear them when they cry out to Him. "I Cried, and He Heard Me" addresses this topic head-on. This book is serious about transforming lives by pointing them to the One who does the transforming.

In the following pages of this book, you will read the real-life stories of women who were in difficult circumstances when they cried out to God for help. Their stories will inspire you. The visionary authors Laila Cuoco Miller and Elisa Cuoco Zinn did a fantastic job bringing this book to fruition. As you dive into this incredible book, I encourage you to cry out to God. Then trust His hand through the process. Soak in every word on these pages, and you will be a changed person on the other side. God is faithful to keep you on the path to destiny.

--Dr. Pamela Henkel
International Best Selling Author, Coach, Mentor,
Philanthropist

I Cried, and He Heard Me

A Collaboration Presented by:
Laila Cuoco Miller & Elisa Cuoco Zinn

Published By: Igniting The Flame Publishing

Library of Congress Cataloging-in-Publication Data has been applied for

ISBN: 9798372311732

PRINTED IN THE UNITED STATES OF AMERICA

To our Parents
Rev. Joseph and Herborg Cuoco:

Thank you for showing us by example,
how to walk through
the FIRE, the STORMS, and the VALLEYS
with your eyes steady on Jesus.
Your lives have been a living testament of
the power of prayer and faith.
You have instilled in us
an immovable foundation of both truth and faith
built on the Rock of our Salvation.
You are and always have been
a beautiful example of what it means to be
Worshippers in Spirit and in Truth.
In doing so,
you have led us straight to
the feet of JESUS.

*T*his book was birthed from a realization that many women are feeling alone in their tears, in their dark seasons, and left wondering if God hears their cries. Our desire was to get a compilation of God-Stories from women all over America. Women who have been through the dark and lonely nights and watched God do what only He can do: Restore, Heal, and Set-Free! This book is a handbook of encouragement that we pray will encourage you, dear reader, to say, "if He did it for her, He can do it for me!"

Who is SorellaLIVE?

We are The Cuoco Sisters, teamed up to unite Women from all ethnic backgrounds. A ministry dedicated to bringing a message of hope and equipping women to walk confidently in Christ. Laila and Elisa are making appearances on radio, television, magazine articles, preach at women's conferences, and now authoring books to reach women all over the world.

SorellaLIVE is passionate about teaching women how to move mountains by using the word of God and the power of prayer.

Table of Contents

Foreword
By Lynette Lewis

*"Do not fear, for I have redeemed you; I have
summoned you by name;*
you are mine*.
When you pass through the waters,
I will be with you;
and when you pass through the rivers,
they will not sweep over you.
When you walk through the fire,
you will not be burned;
the flames will not set you ablaze."*
Isaiah 43:1-2

I can think of nothing more comforting than
knowing our faithful God will never leave us alone;
through every season, storm, or darkness, He
promises to be with us.

When Laila and Elisa asked me to write the
foreword of this book entitled, "I Cried, and He Heard
Me," I knew immediately this book was not only going
to be a book of hope, but it would be used as a key that
would unlock women from living in a place of shame,
hopelessness, and despair. There are so many hearts
needing a reminder of God's faithfulness. And this

anthology will stir faith, pushing those hearts to believe God just a little longer. Reassuring them that if He did it for her, He could do it for me too!

If I could tell you my story, you would hear:
victory over death,
hope over fear, and
faith turned to reality.

You would hear that the hero of my story is my faithful God who, just as He promised, walked with me and never let me drown. I have cried many times, and He always answered. One night in front of my bathroom sink, tears streaming down my cheeks, I heard these words: "Lynette, your story, My glory."

You can trust God. Amidst the questions, the agonies, and the pain. When darkness without even a glimmer prevails. When you look at your accounts and see only withdrawals and even bankruptcy on many levels. Though you've cried out with only apparent silence and zero answers in return. YOU CAN TRUST GOD. He is not asleep but is busy designing. Planning an outcome with ripple effects that reach far beyond your immediate dream—working in you tenacity and perseverance. It takes guts to believe. And you are gutsy and strong. Stronger than you think. And because of all He thinks about you, you will make it.

At times, in the midst of such utter hopelessness, I chose to be a woman of hope. I chose to believe in the faithfulness of God. I know that both Laila and Elisa have had to choose at times to be a woman of hope and to believe in the faithfulness of God.

I pray that as you read through this book's chapters and stories, you will also choose to be a woman of hope.

And then, when you get to the other side, the side of open doors and fresh winds, when answers become evident, and you see above the clouds what was planned all along, at that moment, you will cry again. But this time, not out of desperation. This time thankful that you held on to that tiny little shred of hope and simply chose to believe and be a woman of hope. Women of God - it is YOUR story for His GLORY!

Laila and Elisa are truly forging a path of authentic sisterhood through SorellaLIVE ministries. Their passion for helping women be set free from the lies, strongholds, and fears that threaten to choke out hope and faith is inspiring. I have loved cheering them on while watching the vision of this book turn into reality and bring God's truth and victories to the forefront!

Now I pray that you sit back, open your heart, and allow faith and hope to rise again as you read each story for His glory written in chapters of this anthology!

About - Lynette Lewis

International Speaker, Author, Business Consultant, and Minister

-Helping people know their purpose and fulfill their dream.

Lynette has spoken for major cooperations, including PFIZER, GE, and Johnson & Johnson; has been featured on the TODAY Show, TBN, and other national broadcasts; and is also a

TEDx speaker. This dynamic woman is one of JOHN MAXWELLS Maximum Impact Speakers.

As a Business Consultant, Lynette fills arenas of thousands, speaking on topics including, "The Power of Purpose–Knowing and Loving What You Are Really Meant to Do," and "Building Your Personal Brand and Eminence."

She is the author of the popular New York Post recognized "Climbing the Ladder in Stilettos." As well as "How to Hold Out, Hang On and Marry the Man of Your Dreams."

Lynette Lewis is a DYNAMIC speaker and minister of the Gospel of Jesus, ministering as a keynote speaker at major women's conferences nationwide, such as Gateway Pink Conference, Pure Life NYC & NC, and many more!

Lynette lives a life full of expectation of the power of God in and through her life; she walks confidently in the fulfillment of dreams and seeds sewn for years; she constantly and intrinsically inspires the women around her to reach higher, believe greater, and KNOW our faithful God!

Lynette is married to Pastor Ron Lewis. Together, they have twin young girls, four adult boys, and three grandchildren!

Facebook: Lynette Lewis
instagram: lynettelewis
Website: Lynettelewis.com

Foreword
By Patsy Cameneti

---

n the same way that the phrase "Once Upon a Time" is a typical phrase at the beginning of many children's fiction stories, there is also a key component that marks many of the miracle stories in the Bible. It is that in the darkest and most impossible time, someone cried out to God, and He answered.

I grew up with these exciting stories from the Bible. These were the stories that my siblings and I heard at bedtime, and years later, were the stories I told my own daughters before they went to sleep. Most Bible stories are about an impossible situation or crisis so dreadful that only a miracle from God could help.

Four dark and hopeless situations are described in Psalms 107, and following each plight are these words, "Lord, help!" they cried in their trouble, and he saved them from their distress." There are numerous verses in the Bible that identify this strong characteristic of God of responding to the cry for help.

The many different miracles in the Bible include fulfilled longing for children, healing, provision, deliverance from enemies, storms, death, disaster, and more. The people in these miracle accounts include everyone from kings to slaves, leaders and widows, prophets, military leaders, parents, and basically all kinds of people. The way God brought about the miracle is also unique in each story.

What is remarkable is this God who hears and answers those who cry out is not locked in the Bible but is still doing what only He can do when people cry out to Him.

In I cried, and He Heard Me, Cuoco sisters Laila Miller and Elisa Zinn have compiled powerful real-life stories of twenty eight women who called out to God in the most difficult time of their lives.

While each story is unique, what they all share in common is that each one called to God in their own way and in their own words. And God answered!

I'm sure we've all experienced that when our cry is complaining or directed to different people that nothing changes whatsoever. Let these testimonies inspire you to lift your voice to God. Cry out to Him, using His promises. He hears, and He answers.

"But you, O Lord, are a shield around me; you are my glory, the one who holds my head high. I cried out to the Lord, and he answered me from his holy mountain."

About - Patsy Cameneti

S peaker, Pastor, Missionary, and Author.
Patsy Cameneti has been in full-time ministry since 1977. In her early years, before marriage, Patsy (Behrman) worked with Rev. Kenneth E. Hagin and his ministries. With a strong call and an emphasis on prayer, she directed the Prayer and Healing Center and taught as an instructor at Rhema Bible Training College.

Later, alongside her husband Tony, they directed Bible Schools on three continents; Italy,

Singapore, and Brisbane, Australia. They currently are the Lead Pastors of Rhema Family Church and are Directors of Rhema Bible Training College in both Australia and Papua New Guinea. Additionally, they have an orphanage in Kathmandu, Nepal. Yearly they travel all over the world, speaking at churches and conferences of every kind.

Patsy's message remains fresh and vibrant. Her life and ministry have been marked by a significant truth – the finished work of Christ. Her ministry, therefore, not only reflects Jesus and His redeeming work but demonstrates practically how that truth impacts each believer's daily life and walk with God.

*IG: camenetiministries
*FB: Patsy Cameneti
*Website: https://www.cameneti.net/

FEATURED AUTHOR

Destiny Awaits You
By Jen Tringale

Destiny. Everyone has one but will they live it? That is the eternal question staring each one of us in the face. Not just our overall destiny but our day-to-day destiny. The plans we make, the roads we take, and the words we say.

It is all woven into the fabric that makes this earth go around. Each one of us carries such intricacies in the plan of God that if we knew, it would overwhelm us. But the infinite Master of planning and timing stands outside of time and trusts us. He, God, trusts the power of our new birth in Him that puts us in oneness with Him to carry us through and get each of us to the finish line.

I am being equipped for this even now, and so are you. We are forever growing and becoming the fullness of who He made us to be. That is the journey of life. This is the experiential part. It is the adventure of life's daily potential. To live and breathe and move and have our being in who we are in Him. The only word to describe it is "grand." Some days may not look or feel grand at all, but the painter paints on.

So wait before you take stock of your day or even your life and despair because the painter is not done. He switches His brush stroke, taking the depths of the blacks, the gray, and midnight blues, bringing them into the brighter hues. The contrast of the two is what makes the whole piece in the eye of the beholder awe-struck in wonder. How did He do that with what looked so bleak? Because that is how it is in the hands of God, the Master of destiny. He holds secrets for turning darkness into light.

The myths surrounding hard places in life have plagued people for years, even those who would call themselves Christians. Some have said that God causes bad things to happen so that we will learn, achieve or come to some epiphany of truth. But this is a myth that is untrue. God, by nature, is good. He has given us His word and His spirit to teach, lead and guide us. What He does is look for the entrance into hard places to take advantage of them and work good out of it on our behalf. The truth is, there is a big difference between architecting something harmful and redeeming something that is harmful. But in this redeeming work, He needs our cooperation.

As a woman in full-time public ministry for over 27 years now, I have had my fair share of hard places. So I'd like to share some tools in my tool belt from lessons learned, having been in them and coming through.

The first thing I can tell you is that living stuck in the "why is this happening" or "why did this happen" only delays things for you. God is not thrown by your question, but the essence of the question is pointing a finger and second-guessing His character and goodness. The intellects demand to understand "why" something is happening. I have learned if you go there, you will get stalled. I had to learn to push past my flesh demands for "Why," stay on God's side about it and get to the "Ok, God, what next?"

The best lessons for getting through hard places, especially for leaders, are found in a short story in the book of Acts 28. Paul the Apostle was on a ship that wrecked, and all of the passengers swam to an island nearby called the Island of Malta. A small island off the south coast of Italy. Being Italian is just another reason why I like this story! The people of Malta came out to the shore and greeted them with great kindness and hospitality. This is something Italians are typically known for! They began making a fire for passengers, and Paul went to gather some extra firewood. Side note, a true sign of a mature leader, you are never too important to serve. Now here is where we pick up the story in scripture....

"When Paul had gathered a bundle of sticks and put them on the fire, a viper came out because of the heat and fastened on his hand....He, however, shook off the creature into the fire and suffered no harm."

Think about how random this looks. Paul is doing nothing wrong, living for God, even on a mission trip at the direct leading of the Lord, survives a shipwreck, and now while trying to serve, a poisonous snake comes out of the heat and fastens its venomous fangs into his hand.

I would imagine if you're reading this book, you have experienced life when the heat gets turned up. Pressure is mounting; the climate you are living in seems to be anti-God, maybe even feels "anti-you" and what you're trying to live for. Maybe you've had venomous words said about you. People you thought were with you turned on you or simply walked away—attacks on every side. And maybe right when you were walking out of one shipwreck experience in life, another hit came seemingly out of nowhere.

Make no mistake about it, friend. You have to see it for what it is and what is really going on. The enemy of your life is trying to get you off track and disheartened.

There is always war at the gates of your destiny. Recognizing this is transformative in how you deal with it. Being aware of the enemy's devices will help you hold your ground in your soul and find your strength in the Lord.

What Paul did next is the key to coming through all those hard places. The Bible says when the snake lept at him, and the bite came, He shook it off. I have learned when the heat gets turned up, and an attack comes at you, and it looks like it has the ability to take you out...shake it off. Now I don't say this lightly as if to say, "Oh, it's no big deal." These attacks were serious and real; Paul's life was at stake. But He knew what to do. He had to shake it off so that his soul didn't go into fear, panic, and despondency.

There is a maturing and growing to handle hard places in life. At first, most of us do not handle it well.

But the Lord is calling us to a higher place, especially in this day and time we are living in. To walk with Him even in the midst of the hard places and the attack, all so that He can work His wonders in our midst.

What was the outcome of Paul's hard place? It says, "He suffered no harm."

God didn't send the snake, the serpent of lies sent that snake, but God was able to have entered into that scenario because of what Paul chose to do. Shake it off.

The people were so amazed that the viper's venom not only didn't take Paul out but didn't even make him ill that the governor of the island invited Paul into his home. There Paul prayed for his father-in-law, who was healed, which led to Paul staying on that island for three months preaching and miracles took place. The Lord redeemed and used what the enemy meant for harm. That is what your God always desires to do with you. So let me say this to you, don't give up!

Your God has the ability to work wonders in the midst of the plots your enemy weaves against you. Stay on God's side. Shake it off. Don't let it get into your soul. Don't get stuck in the questions. Be strong in the Lord and in the power of His might. The power of the Holy Spirit will rise up inside you and enable you to shake it off once you choose this as your response.

Woman of God, you are a woman of great purpose. You have authority. Use it when hard places come. If you get your faith in agreement with God, He will take the grays and the dark blues of life and work them into a stunning exhibition of His artistry on the canvas of your life. Who can wait to see what the day holds when He rides upon the darkest night? Truly, great is our God. Let me pray over you.

Father, I lift up my sister to you as she is reading this, and I pray that you would remove any effects of hurtful words spoken to her, against her, or about her. Those scheming words for her failure I call down in the name of Jesus. What the enemy plots for evil towards her, I declare that she is strong and will suffer no harm. God, right now, shift the words, the experiences, all of the hard places that brought such hurt into deep wells of healing until there is no hurt remaining.

I release restoration to her in all the ways she needs it right now, in Jesus' name. I pray that as she reads the stories and testimonies in these pages that a fresh boldness and vitality will take hold of her on the inside and propel her into greater strength, greater faith, and greater vision than she has known before.

I declare over you that your destiny awaits you. Your future is bright. Right now in your life, a new day is dawning. In Jesus' name, I pray. Amen.

About - Jen Tringale

en Tringale is an internationally known speaker, author, and strategist on awakening destiny. She is known for her integration of purpose, innovation, faith, and spirituality. Her messaging reaches across cultures and vocations to unlock the purpose and potential within individuals, organizations, cities, and nations. Her reach includes a robust international speaking schedule, her books "Your Defining Moment" and "Calling," and a podcast that opened in iTunes' Top 40 charts with an audience of over 200,000 listeners in more than fifty nations. Her international influence includes meetings with Heads of State, Cabinet Members, the U.S. Embassy, and State Department Representatives. In 2016 she hosted a history-making, nationwide women's conference in the nation of Grenada. It was the first of its kind, with thousands in attendance, including dignitaries and prominent leaders. After over twenty years of ministry, Jen is positioned as a leading voice in the current generation who communicates with clarity, boldness, and passion on divine destiny and bringing Jesus Christ into culture. Her initiatives to equip and empower extend beyond the pulpit and pew into every arena of culture for an influential shift. She has appeared on television networks such as TBN, TCT, the Believers Voice of Victory Network and has been featured in the Word of Faith Magazine. Jen is a graduate of Rhema Bible College and is originally from Florence, KY. She embraces both her southern roots and Italian heritage and now resides in Nashville, TN.

IG: @Jentringale
FB: Jentringale
www.jentringale.com

FEATURED AUTHOR

He Was There
By Lisa Max

I came out of the womb naked, hungry, and crying like every other newborn baby. However, it didn't take long for me to become separated from the others. Where other little girls went home to affectionate embraces, eye gazes, and being fussed over, my cries were seldom heard. With a one and two-year-old already demanding my mother's time and attention, my needs seemed to have pushed something away deep inside her that would never return.

No matter how many times my mom told the story, I never saw the humor in putting a newborn baby in the bathtub as a crib substitute. It wasn't until I became a mother myself that I saw the harshness of laying a tender-skinned baby who couldn't yet lift her head in a cold, hard, sterile porcelain bathtub for hours every day. As the high white walls consumed my tiny body, I soon learned my cries fell on deaf ears. I stopped crying at an early age and was aware I was placed outside of my own family.

My mother was on her own journey of unpacking her childhood owies where she encountered hard, harsh, and cold responses from her parents, who were heavily into the occult. She, too, learned that she was on her own in this big world. She found her value in being successful and achieving greatness in front of the classroom and was named Teacher of the Year for decades. To this day, she holds the title of "favorite teacher" to many. My mother had a unique talent and ability to pour into children who weren't her own that never transferred to the family room.

There was something about me that reminded her of what she longed to ignore. My mere existence triggered her. No little girl has the capacity to comprehend why her presence caused her own mother to recoil. It would take me the next 40 years for my heart to understand that it wasn't about me personally but that she was on her own journey dealing with a heart full of splinters.

I adored my dad and felt safer with him. When I was five, my parents divorced; I was livid. I already learned tears were pointless and didn't get heard, but I realized that anger was an easy emotion for me to express. I missed him terribly, yet even my grief, as crooked as it was, pushed her away even further.

My mom approached me one day and told me she was taking me out for dinner. We barely said a word all night, but I could tell you exactly what little five-year-old me wore, what we ordered, and how many glasses of water I drank. It was a unique experience to spend alone time with my mother, yet I had to convince myself she wanted to be there despite her communicating otherwise.

She announced at the end of dinner that she was taking me to a doctor, which confused me as I didn't feel sick. We drove in the cold Minnesota winter night and walked into what felt more like a house than a doctor's office. I could not figure out why there were no waiting room chairs or receptionists like in my pediatrician's office. It was eerie to me that it was at night as I had only gone to the doctor during the day. Then it came. The question that would haunt me for decades and nearly take my life. My mom asked, "Did your dad ever ____" in the name of sexual abuse. I was dumbfounded and wildly uncomfortable. While I valued the unfamiliar attention she was giving me, having to allow my mind to actually consider what she was saying was confusing.

I have a photographic memory and can recall the smallest of details from my past, so to have this looming question hang over me was haunting. Why couldn't my mind tell me the truth about what happened? Where did it happen? Or worse yet, why did it happen? Each day I would strain my brain to reveal the truth that everyone was waiting for me to confess.

The crying may have stopped, but the trauma didn't. I learned about suicide in the 4th grade while watching a television show, and it dawned on me that this is what one is *supposed* to do with their pain. I went to the cupboard and grabbed whatever medicine I could find, not even thinking about death. One of my siblings went to the bathroom to round up the rest of the medicine in our house and said, "Do us a favor. Keep going."

So I did. For the next two decades, I was plagued with an addiction to suicide. I hated my brain for not telling me the truth about my dad. I feared more, not knowing rather than the reality of whatever horror my dad did to me. Self-hatred became a lifestyle; I simply began to treat the girl in the mirror the way I watched my mother treat her for years.

My 24-year-old lifeless body lay in bed for three full days before my roommate barged in, ignoring the 'do not disturb' sign on the door. She found my gray skin doubled in size from the built-up toxins due to my liver shutting down. While on the phone with 911, she noticed the scores of prescription bottles littered all over my bedroom floor.

The first officer on the scene called me DOA - dead on arrival, but the second officer triumphed, announcing, "I found a faint pulse." I love that part of my story because life and light always trump death and darkness. I was rushed to the hospital, where I would spend the next three months fighting for my life in a coma. When I woke up, the first thing they told me was that my mother had died the month before, and I missed the funeral and burial. The second thing they told me was that I had 85% hearing loss from the drugs in my system and was currently on the waiting list for not one but two transplants. The concoction of pills I consumed to swallow my tears had destroyed my liver and kidneys.

My body was filled with tubes to put the good stuff in and to pump out the bad. I was on a feeding tube, breathing machine, and dialysis. For months I was too weak to go to the bathroom alone, let alone brush my teeth. So I just laid there, day in and day out, pushing back the pain that was trying so hard to be heard.

As I lay in my hospital bed surrounded by walls covered in get-well cards, someone gave me a Hallmark card that read, "With God on your side, you will never be alone." I knew at that moment I had missed the boat. I was raised knowing God but not experiencing Him. I was alone. Very alone. I had lost the woman I would never gain as a mother. The cells in my body cried out for her nurturing embrace, a mother's kiss, and the comfort of her tender hands that I had longed for every day yet never knew. Instead, I was met with the reality that I was indeed all alone; I felt bankrupt and left completely empty. I was convinced I would never know comfort on this side of heaven.

I began to cry another cry, a hunger in my soul so deep I thought I would die of starvation. I broke down and let out decades of pent-up tears, reminding Him that my heart was shattered into a bazillion pieces but that I believed in Him and that He could have my life. I told Him that I didn't just want to live a life knowing Him; I wanted to be a poster child that He is powerful. Shortly after, the doctors came in to remove me from dialysis and then the kidney transplant list. A week later, to the amazement of my entire medical team, they removed me from the liver transplant list. He was showing Himself as powerful.

Months later, my sister reluctantly shared that I was unresponsive to all touch while in my coma.

Despite being estranged from my father at the time, he rushed to my side when he learned of his daughter's near-death state. My sister went on to say that when he walked into the room, my body began to react. When I heard his voice, I began thrashing around on the bed, causing the nurses to be greatly concerned. I had such a violent physical reaction that they called security, and he was ushered out with a strong warning never to return.

Tears rolled down my cheeks when she told me, and I remember telling her I thought they got it wrong. I wasn't responding because I was upset; I was responding because I was a daughter who deeply longed for her daddy in her time of need, and he came. I believe I was reacting because I felt his love.

He was there.

Like most people who endure a near-death experience, there are things that need to be processed. At the time, I wasn't a believer when I died three times, and they brought me back, yet I vividly recall the experience. My mentor asked Jesus to show me where He was when I was dying. I was so offended that she would ask where a Holy God was in the midst of my darkest hour. I didn't believe He would stoop so low as to be in the midst of my utter chaos and greatest sin. She showed me Romans 5:8, which revealed He was there. I closed my eyes and asked, "Jesus, where were You?" and saw me lying on my hospital bed with Jesus by my feet. His elbows were holding up His face buried in the palm of His hands. I was so taken aback by the mere revelation that He was there. While it didn't change my reality, it changed everything to realize I was never alone because He was there. My mentor sensed there was more He wanted to show me and asked Him, "Jesus, what were You doing by Lisa's bedside?" I saw His face begin to lift from His hands. His eyes were tear-stained; He was crying. Crying like a faithful parent watching His daughter in so much pain, crying that she was taking the sins of another upon herself. Crying that she doesn't know who she is. He was crying because of what sin and death do to His beloved creation.

He was there.

Aren't we all just sons and daughters who want to know daddy came for us in our hour of need?

Friends, Jesus is there!

P.S. Years later, in an inner healing session, we asked Holy Spirit to reveal the truth about what my dad had done to me, and He clearly showed me nothing happened. We had seven glorious years of reconciliation together before he passed away. It would take me another ten years to forgive my deceased mother, but God ended up birthing a ministry through me to help other parents. It is my love offering back to my mother to give other parents the tools she needed to parent me but never had.

About - Lisa Max

Lisa Max is a mom who began ushering her children to the Father at an early age, where He became an everyday part of their family. She is now the director of Let the Children Fly, an Apostolic Hub for families that empowers families around the globe to partner with Holy Spirit in their parenting. She is passionately dedicated to equipping families to pick up their family mantle, which includes walking in authority, building solid connections, and healing from childhood heart splinters. Lisa, along with her four children, loves to play in the Kingdom and ignite fires in others to do the same.

Connect with Lisa
Facebook -
LettheChildrenFly (https://www.facebook.com/groups/
Letthechildrenfly)

Website - LettheChildrenFly
(www.LettheChildrenFly.com)

Instagram - LettheChildrenFly

VISIONARY AUTHOR

Look at Me Now
By Laila Cuoco Miller

—⁓⁓⁓—

When you are in the middle of the storm and facing your darkest hours, sometimes you think, this is it. It is the end. How will God ever be able to turn my life around?

I had a chapter, a season in my life just like that. Moments of staring out my window, watching neighbors in their homes wondering what their lives were like. Were they happy? Were they struggling like me? Moments of planning how I could save myself, break out of the box, break out of the depression that made me see only DARKNESS. It was horrible. I was a minister's daughter, a minister myself, and married to a minister. I was supposed to be perfect! But I was not. I was broken and falling apart! I needed help and didn't know how to fix it myself. I found myself CRYING OUT to God in despair.

Have you ever felt that way or found yourself in a situation where you were crying out, HOW can I get through this? If so, I pray this chapter stirs faith in your heart that if He did it for me, He WILL do it for you! Psalm 18:6 says, "In my distress, I called to the Lord, I cried to God for help. He heard my voice, my cry came before him, into his ears."

Things worsened when my marriage ended in an ugly divorce. I ended up losing everything: my family, my ministry, and my home. Everything I had identified myself with was gone. I found myself now as a single mom. I did not know what I would do for work because I only knew ministry. I had given everything to God, and my life revolved around our ministry. How could this possibly happen? WHY God? It was not God's fault. But, at that time, I took my disappointment out on Him. I felt lost and abandoned. I was devastated and decided I was done with God! So, I made a couple of decisions. I was going to re-invent myself and moving forward; I was going to do things MY way!

In the following years, I lived my life angry at God. Occasionally I would go to church and would sit in the back where no one could see me and just weep uncontrollably. As angry as I was at God, He always met me there, reaching down and grabbing hold of my broken heart. The truth is, wherever I was, there God was also. His mercy was upon my life. He continually showed up so gently in unusual ways just to remind me of His love. Yes, HE heard my cries. The word of God says, "The righteous cry out, and God hears our cries!" Psalm 34:17. No matter what you are going through, your situation may look dark and impossible in your eyes, but when you cry out as a daughter of God, HE WILL HEAR YOU! He does not ignore you.

Having to start all over again, I was determined to stick to my new plan. I enrolled and went back to college. One day as I was walking on campus, a modeling scout approached me and gave me her card. Shortly after, I started modeling. I figured it was a good plan for the extra money. But modeling introduced me to a whole new world. An exciting world, so it seemed at that moment. I enjoyed doing fashion shows, calendar shoots, and other exciting modeling events. I met producers, famous actors, and famous athletes. I thought I was really enjoying life and doing it my way!

However, I was a sheltered girl who, now in my thirties, would learn what life without God really looked like. And let me tell you, life without God would quickly introduce itself to me! With modeling came the after-parties and the lifestyle of money and drugs. Thankfully, none of this ever enticed me, but I saw things I had never seen before. I saw what sin could do. Money can never buy happiness, leaving so many with a void they thought fame and fortune could fill. The fame, the money, and lavish lifestyles can never give the peace and fulfillment that Jesus can. I noticed the lonely faces and the emptiness many expressed in conversation. Strangely enough, backslidden, and mad at God, I found my heart compelled me to share Jesus, and I would pray with people at these events!

God would not give up on me. He continued to gently reach out to me with reminders of His love and His mercy. I will never forget one encounter where the Lord took me totally by surprise! I had taken my son to Norway for his 16th birthday. We visited some of our family there and did some sightseeing together. As we were at a train station in Norway waiting for the next train to arrive, a gentleman sat down next to us. What caught my eye was that he sat there with his guitar case next to him. He said, HELLO. I said hello back. I continued to talk to my son. I had no intention of talking to a stranger. But apparently, this stranger had a plan and started talking to me. I was very skeptical, but he drew me into a conversation by telling me he was on his way to Africa to preach and lead worship with his guitar! I replied, no way! My father is in Mozambique at this very moment preaching. He also sings and plays the guitar!

God sure knew what would catch my attention! What were the odds I would meet a man in Norway, traveling to Africa with his guitar at the SAME time my father was traveling there!? After a short conversation, I then turned my attention back to my son. The gentleman tapped me on the shoulder and said, I have a message for you. The Lord wants me to relay it to you. I rolled my eyes - ugh! I absolutely did not want some random stranger to "prophecy" over me! That was the last thing I wanted! He asked, would you please allow me to share it with you? My son then turned to me and said, Mom, just let him tell you. So, I agreed. AND BAM! He started reading my life. He told me my thoughts, my plans, and my frustrations. EVERY detail was read to me aloud there in that train station.

I broke down crying. My heart had become so hardened that it was years since I had cried. But God was there speaking directly to me. My Son Pauly was also surprised and in awe! In the end, we exchanged a few words and said our goodbyes as the train was arriving. My son and I got up to head toward the train. As we did, we took one more look back to say goodbye to this stranger, and he was GONE! He was nowhere to be found! And then I realized, "Be not forgetful to entertain strangers: for thereby some have entertained angels unawares." Hebrews 13:2

God had not forgotten me. He was so concerned about me that he set up a divine encounter to hear from HIM through a messenger. I believe this stranger was an angel. Pauly and I were in shock! We could not stop talking about what had just happened the entire train ride home and shared the story with our family.

I was the one sheep that left the fold, and HE came searching for me! Yes, HE cared enough about me to search me out. He left the 99 to come to find me all the way in Norway!

After our amazing trip to Norway, we returned home to the States, where I resumed my lifestyle of everything that was the opposite of living for God. Yet this time, I felt a stirring in my heart and knew I had to make changes; I just didn't know how.

My father being the man of God that he is, spoke into my life, telling me it was time to make changes. He was the final nudge it took to finally walk away from this lifestyle that had taken me so far from the girl I once was. So, I packed my bags. Both my parents helped my sweet son and me to move to another State. It was the beginning of another chapter.

Looking back, I am so thankful I had loving parents who were always there for me. Godly parents who prayed for me! My parents held onto the word concerning me, Proverbs 22:6, "train up a child in the way they should go and when they grow old, they will not depart from it." They knew it was a promise that would come to pass. My parents watched me walk away from God, angry and full of hurt. They watched me live an ungodly life and still stood by me. They loved me unconditionally. Oh, how my precious parents faithfully prayed and interceded for me. They were a constant reminder of HIS unfailing love.

Shortly after I had moved, I received horrifying news about a family member who I had spent most of my time with before moving away. I loved this person dearly. Tragedy! She had taken her own life, and I was devastated. The news cut me to the core. I felt as if hopelessness had enveloped me, and I was spiraling. Oh, how I cried out to God. How did I not see this coming?

Devastated from losing this person, I broke down one night on my bedroom floor and had a heart-to-heart with God. I made a deal with Him. It was an I cried, and HE heard me moment! I finally opened my heart back up to God. And ohhhh, what a glorious turn my life took after that! Slowly my life began to come together in such a beautiful way. The hand of God began to cause my life to blossom, and the Lord began to restore to me ALL that was once stolen.

Fast forward years later, I found myself driving up to the house where this all started. The house of pain. The house where my marriage was falling apart. The house where I was burning out on ministry. The house where depression and hopelessness set in. This was the place where I hit rock bottom and could only see the dark. I drove up, looked at THAT house, and with tears of joy streaming down my face, I said out loud, "LOOK AT ME NOW." I am a new person! I am happy, complete, loved, believed in, and blessed on all levels of my life! BUT GOD. He saw, and He knew all along.

As I am writing this, I reflect on how life can throw so many twists and turns. But more amazing is how GOD sees the end of each season, the end of each chapter! Dear beautiful woman, reading this right now. I am here to tell you HE has not forgotten you. He hears your cries even when others do not. The word of God says in Psalm 107:6, "They cried out to God, and HE rescued them!"

And so, you too will walk out from amongst the fire, the smoke lingering around you, as the ashes from the flames fall to the wayside. You will continue to walk forward, focused on what is ahead. The Holy Spirit will breathe on you like gusts of wind rushing over you, creating a feeling of renewal and refreshing. And so, it will begin a new chapter of what is to be. You, too, will look back and say, Look at Me NOW!

About Visionary Author
Laila Cuoco Miller

Laila (Cuoco) Miller began in full-time ministry as a young girl of 19 years of age and has continued in various forms of ministry for the past 35 years. She has served as Associate Pastor, pioneered her own church, and has traveled nationally & internationally preaching and teaching the word of God.

Walking in her prophetic gifting, Laila's love for people motivates her to practice His presence on the daily as she is prompted to reach out to people outside of the church with God's love and healing power! She calls these her "God Encounters."

Laila is the co-founder and visionary of SorellaLIVE Ministries. She and her sister Elisa are reaching women with a message of hope and teaching women how to walk life out boldly using God's word & the power of prayer. Their ministry has allowed them to speak to women all over the world through a podcast, virtual meetings, and in person at churches as well as other platforms.

Laila has earned two degrees and is an Ordained Minister, bestselling Author, and Certified Life Coach.

Laila and her husband, Jeff, as entrepreneurs, currently run two successful businesses together. In their free time, they enjoy traveling and surrounding themselves with their beautiful family. As they say in Italian - La Famiglia e Tutto! (Family is Everything)

Contact Laila at: Sorellaministries@gmail.com

You can follow Laila on:
IG: sorella.live
FB: Sorella LIVE
Website: sorellaministries.live

VISIONARY AUTHOR

"Your Will, Your Way"
My Prayer in the Waiting
By Elisa Cuoco Zinn

Take courage my heart, stay steadfast my soul
He's in the waiting
He's in the waiting
Hold on to your hope, as your triumph unfolds
He's never failing
He's never failing

"Wait for the Lord; be strong, and let your heart take
courage; wait for the Lord!
Psalms 27:14

W aiting is hard. It is long and sometimes lonely. We wonder where He is as we wander around in what seems like a holding pattern. The reality is that we don't have to look far. He is IN the waiting. You see, He doesn't place us in seasons of waiting to put us on time-out without Him. He places us in these seasons to pull us close to Him. When all we have is our hope and faith, He is

THERE. He longs for us to draw near to Him. Because when we do, we become a little more like Him, reflecting His glory. Waiting may be hard, but in my experience, it is the most beautiful of seasons.

I speak from experience, as it seems that every large area of my life has been marked with a waiting period. These times have tested my obedience and faith while simultaneously producing a deeper love and intimacy for my Jesus.

Like many, I was a little girl dreaming big dreams. I had dreams of marrying my perfect prince, being a mother of six (or maybe ten) children, and ministering alongside my tall, dark, handsome husband while preaching the Gospel in many nations. I was SURE these dreams were God-inspired, so, of course, He would be faithful to make them a reality for me. However, what really happened was watching EACH. DREAM. DIE. Then after seasons of waiting, I would watch God resurrect them into a new glorious reality.

I grew up in a loving, God-fearing family. I was the youngest of four. My parents were pastors, but more importantly, they were worshippers of Jesus. They sang and worshipped together, filling our home with songs of faith. We sang and worshipped together as a family. My father led us from his guitar. This instilled in us a heart of worship as we learned how to tap into the presence of God and how to worship through life's difficult moments. I loved and served God all my life. I was zealous for the things of God and very careful to follow God's will and not to make mistakes in my choices.

I sought God for where I would go to college, what I would major in and who I would date. I dated a few times and would end the relationship knowing that God said "NO."

I spent the majority of my 20s single, traveling and living in Europe on the mission field. One night, while living in Italy, I was mopping the floor, minding my own thoughts, and the Holy Spirit dropped on me like a blanket of conviction. He began to deal with me about submitting to Him in a specific area of my life. I knelt down and began to cry, wrestling with the conviction of the Holy Spirit. It was time to submit my will to His in that area, but I really didn't want to. As I was praying, this prayer bubbled up right out of my spirit, "YOUR WILL, and YOUR WAY." It was this phrase that would become the prayer anchor of my life.

He was teaching me that it wasn't just about following His will, but He wanted me to submit to the WAY He was going to bring His will to pass in my life.

As I approached my late 20s, I saw that I was nowhere near what I had planned in my mind. I looked around and saw friends dating and marrying easily, without bleeding in prayer, asking God if this was His will! I decided that if everyone else could do it, so could I! I would take things into my own hands, date a normal Christian guy, get married, and get this dream on its feet.

That plan didn't turn out so well. I began to date someone I met at a Bible study (pretty safe). We dated for a while, and although it was fun, deep down, I knew this relationship was not God's best for either of us. I pushed on, convincing myself it would be fine. We got engaged and planned a wedding. In the meantime, unbeknownst to me, my parents and siblings were praying and fasting for me. They knew this was not God's best and asked Him to end this relationship before it was too late. Four weeks before the wedding, when my dress was bought, bridesmaid dresses altered, plane tickets for guests checked...I could no longer reconcile the churning in my spirit, and I called it off.

Talk about a low place. There I was, broken-hearted, embarrassed, and staring into the abyss of a blank future.

"What now, God? Where are you in this?"

(I'm in the waiting)

Weeping, I repented for taking matters into my own hands and submitted my will to His again. "Your will YOUR way, God."

It was at this point God connected me with a new church plant in Times Square, NYC. A church was planted right after the twin towers went down. The word given to Founding Pastor Ron Lewis was, "Out of the ashes, I will build my church." I knew those ashes were referring to the horrific attack on our country and the lives that were lost. Yet that year, I felt I was also rising from the ashes to be built into a temple that would glorify Him alone. The very first service I attended, I knew I was home. Worship enveloped my heart, and I wept again in His presence that night, reminded of how good God was to me and that I could trust Him. I packed up my things and moved to NYC to be a part of this church. I always say that God used the big vast city of New York to be an incubator of His presence in my life. He worked on my heart and set me on my feet again.

In that year, He also gave me a beautiful redemptive picture of my dream of marriage. This was from the book of Ruth, as a promise to tuck in my heart, reminding me His way is yet to come. As Ruth was working in the same field as Boaz, so my husband would be in the same field as me as we build His kingdom together.

About a year later, this NYC church had plans to plant a church in the Philadelphia/South Jersey region. That was where I grew up, and my parents pastored a church. Even though my family had moved a few years before this, that area always felt like "home" to me. One night during a worship service, the Lord spoke so clearly to my heart, saying, "I'm sending you back to the area your family planted and worked in. It's time to GO." So I packed up and headed back, as part of a team, to plant what is now known as Freedom Church Philadelphia.

One man who was a part of this team was a friend from years past. He was a businessman who had a heart hungry to see a move of God in our area. He was also a tall, good-looking Italian, which would have normally set my heart swooning. But a businessman? That didn't fit the dream. In *my* dream, my husband would be in the fivefold ministry. But God gently reminded me of the beautiful picture He gave me of Ruth working in the same field as her ***businessman*** husband (Ha! Ha! Somehow, I had missed that part of the story!) It took some time for our love story to form, but God is always in the middle of our submitted time. At 35 years old, God answered the prayer of my heart - His way.

We were married in a beautiful church, on a glorious summer's day, with our family and friends celebrating God's goodness on us and for us! Even better, a year later, we found out we were pregnant! Filled with excitement, I just knew God was blessing our hearts that were submitted to Him. He was breathing into our dreams and bringing the next part into reality!

Pictures of ultrasounds taped onto our bathroom mirror, speaking God's word over this new life. Names swirling around, hoping boy or girl, dreaming of all the joys to come. Telling our friends and families, who joined in the dance of excitement.

Until a routine doctor visit showed there was no longer a heartbeat.

The room went still, and my heart froze. I couldn't hear anything after the doctor said those words. My mind could barely grasp what he was saying. Your will Your way? God, was THIS your way? Haven't I waited? Submitted? Obeyed? I couldn't understand how God could let this happen!

"GOD? Where are you?!"

(I'm in the waiting)

Tears streaming down my face, I submitted my will again to Him. I fell at His feet and worshipped Him. He is faithful, and in His presence, I was reminded again that I could trust Him. No matter what I saw in the natural, I could trust Him to bring about His purpose for my life... His way.

Grieving, the doctors tried to explain that we were at "advanced maternal age."

ADVANCED MATERNAL AGE? So now, it seemed that having ONE child would be a miracle. What about my dream of having six?

Before we knew it, we were swimming in a swirl of fertility procedures. Blood tests every other day, shots, ultrasounds, pills, more shots, negative reports. For two years. Month after month, waiting, trusting, believing. My biological clock was ticking as each test was NEGATIVE.

"GOD, where are you?"

(I'm in the waiting)

We found ourselves at the altar, holding hands, tears streaming down our faces, and desperate for God to move. Our spiritual family circled around us, praying over us, Oh, that we would see Your faithfulness in all of the grief!

It was November, and we had done enough of other fertility options to satisfy insurance quotas. IVF was set for the end of the month. I said, "God, I know you use IVF to bring life. However, YOU are the author of life. I recognize that if IVF is not your WAY for me, I'll still trust you."

Hopeful, I went in for step one of IVF only to hear the doctor tell me I could not advance. My body had produced a cyst from the prior fertility medicines and needed to wait until the next month. Great. Time out for me again. More waiting time.

"GOD, where are You?

(I'm in the waiting)

I had learned to meet Him there, in the waiting. Sweet times of worship, sitting in His presence in the midst of my pain, brought renewed hope. Hope against hope.

Remembering the stories of Abraham, "Without weakening in his faith, he faced the fact that his body was as good as dead—since he was about a hundred years old—and that Sarah's womb was also dead. Yet he did not waver through unbelief regarding the promise of God, but was strengthened in his faith and gave glory to God, being fully persuaded that God had power to do what he had promised." Romans 4:21

The next IVF date was set for December 26th.

HOPE AGAINST HOPE.

In early December, I had some strange signs in my cycle. Hesitantly, I took a pregnancy test. Was that a second line we saw? Using a flashlight, it was there. Faint but it was there.

I WAS PREGNANT, and it happened naturally! Dispelling every lie and torment, God did His miracle-working power in my body!

How we cried tears of JOY! My God is faithful! At 38 years old, I held my beautiful baby boy. And just when they thought it wouldn't happen, God gave us another beautiful baby boy when I was 39! Then at 40, I carried my precious baby girl. Three children naturally in three years! Only God!

His will, His Way.

As the next years flew by, filled with mothering and homeschooling, I started to feel the tug again for ministry. This part of my dream had been at a standstill. The desire to step into ministry in a greater capacity was stirring. During these years, I kept active as one of our church's worship leaders, discipled women, led Bible studies, and prayed for and with people, but the call of God on my life to preach and teach the Gospel was awakening again. However, there didn't seem to be a "place at the table" for me. I began to feel overlooked and forgotten. With my feelings of inadequacy, I would run to the Father and spend time with Him in worship. He would remind me again of my call, His anointing on my life, and that it was He who called me, not man. I could trust His timing to open doors for me. He was in the waiting.

It was around this same point my "businessman husband" began to recognize a call to ministry in a capacity different than before. God then began to use us together. Unfolding gifts of the spirit that complimented the other. He opened moments and space at our home church for us to speak and to exhort the body of Christ. We were then commissioned as ministers in the church.

Looking back, I can see the beauty in the dying-to-rebirth of these dreams. God has woven a beautiful tapestry of love, family, and ministry in our lives, yet we know there is more to come. More dreams are in the waiting. While we wait, we worship Him, becoming more like Him day by day.

If you are in a waiting season, I encourage you to find people who will pray with you, find scriptures as promises for you to hold on to, turn on the worship music and get in His presence. It will change your perspective. Let His will and His way be the prayer of your heart as well. Trust Him to make something beautiful in your life!

I cried, and God heard me. He will hear you too.

"I remain confident of this: I will see the goodness of the Lord in the land of the living. Wait for the Lord; be strong and take heart and wait for the Lord."
Psalms 27:13-14

About Visionary
Elisa Cuoco Zinn

Elisa Cuoco Zinn is a dynamic speaker called to awaken and activate FAITH within the heart of the listener, helping them to connect back to the heart of God. She flows intentionally with the Holy Spirit as she ministers uniquely on each platform.

Elisa has worked in the supportive role of many ministries in the last 25 years, both here in the U.S. as well as in various European countries. Both a graduate of North Central University and Rhema Bible Training Center - majoring in Biblical studies/church ministry- she has dedicated her life to building His Kingdom while preaching the Word, leading people in worship, discipling women, and training children to love God.

Following her passion for discipling women, Elisa co-founded, alongside her sister Laila, SorellaLIVE: A ministry dedicated to teaching and equipping women to walk confidently in Christ by using the combined power of the Word of God and PRAYER to move mountains.

Elisa is happily married to Paul Zinn. She fully homeschools their three children: Rocco, Lorenzo, and Valentina. Together they love outdoor adventures, bike rides, hiking, and beach trips.

Contact Elisa
IG: Sorella.LIVE
FB: Elisa Cuoco Zinn
FB Group: SorellaLIVE
Web: Sorellaministries.live

Touched By An Angel
By Tiffany Jones

It was a pang of guilt like none I had ever experienced or have ever since. I was tormented and cried every day for an entire year. I didn't think that God would forgive me. How could He? I couldn't forgive myself. Let me back up and tell you a little about my journey prior to the moment above.

I grew up the child of two unwed teenage parents, raised by their praying mothers. Both of my grandmothers raised me with a fear of the Lord. We went to church every Sunday and a few weekdays too. Yet, even with all of the time I spent in church, I never developed a personal relationship with Christ. I did develop a relationship with going to church. I found myself worshiping my grandmother's God. I survived off of my grandmother's prayers and the residue of their time with the Lord.

I moved away from my hometown of Winston-Salem, N.C., at the age of 12. My mom got married, and my step-father was stationed in V.A. So, off I went to live with them. Sadly, going to church stopped, but the seed had already been planted. I went through my high school years like a typical teenager. Boy crazy, insecure, desperate for attention, seeking approval, driven by a constant need to appear perfect, etc. I was struggling while keeping a smile on my face. My high school years were *HARD*. Things at home were not great. My mom and her husband separated. We were left by him to fend for ourselves. As soon as I could, I got a job to help with bills. My life consisted of school, music, and work. God was not on my mind; However, back in N.C., my grandmothers were praying. They were covering me when I didn't know how to pray for myself.

In the summer of 1994, I moved to Philadelphia to attend Temple University. My family was so excited. I was the first grandchild to go away to a four-year college. Everyone was so proud. During my freshman year, I met the love of my life. We fell for each other fast and hard. We became intimate, and I became pregnant. I was petrified. I was the golden child. I was born to unwed teenage parents. I lived the consequences of unplanned parenthood. Now I was doing the same thing. I could not look my family in the eye and let them down in this way.

I decided to terminate the pregnancy. At the time, the consequence of having a baby seemed greater than not. I had no idea what was about to unfold in my life. The moment the procedure was over, a dark cloud descended above me, and I was consumed with guilt. I returned to my dorm room and began sobbing uncontrollably. I hadn't been to church in years, yet the only name I thought to call was Jesus. I cried out to Him every day. He led me to join the university gospel choir. I was desperately trying to get back to what my grandmothers had shown me. Music has always been where I've felt the closest to God.

In the Spring of the following year, the choir went on tour. While at a small church in North Carolina, my life changed forever. The Spirit of the Lord was tangible. Everyone was worshiping and praising God. While in the choir stand, I was weeping and crying out to God for forgiveness. I could not let go of what I had done. The room became blurry, and time seemed to stop. I saw a woman in all white walking toward me. She said, "Hi, my name is Cathy. Can I sit with you?" Through my sobs, I said, "Yes." She crossed over me and sat to my right. She placed her left arm around my shoulders and her right hand in mine. She said, "God told me to tell you that He forgives you. You can let it go now." I began to sob again. At that moment, I could feel the heaviness falling off of me. She then proceeded to pray with me. This moment felt like an hour, but in reality, it could not have been more than a few minutes. After her prayer, she got up and left the choir stand. I saw her walk to the left. The Pastor's podium was blocking my view, so I couldn't see where she was seated.

After service, I looked for Cathy but could not find her. I asked the young lady that was seated next to me if she saw the woman that came and prayed with me. To my surprise, she said, "What lady? No one came to the choir stand." My heart began to race. Tears filled my eyes. I became warm all over. I was so confused. I asked the young lady behind me. "Did you see the lady that sat and prayed with me?" She also responded,

"What Lady?" Then I realized, He thought enough of me to send an Angel. It was at that moment I stopped serving my Grandmother's God and began my journey of knowing Him for myself. He came for me. I cried out. He heard me!

I have never shared this story publicly. I allowed shame to paralyze me. Would I be able to serve in ministry if people knew? Would they think less of me? What would my family think? Would this change the way that they see me? Well, I have decided that obedience to God is greater than fear of man. This next level of freedom that I am experiencing is indescribable. I now live in a place of victory and authority. I can state that our Father is a redeemer because I've experienced His redemption.

For any of my sisters out there that are walking and living under a cloud of guilt and shame, read 1 John 1:9. The Word says if we confess our sins, He is faithful and just to forgive and cleanse us from all unrighteousness. It is my prayer that by sharing my story, you will come to believe that Jesus is an advocate for us. I am a living, breathing example of Isaiah 61:7. "Instead of your shame there shall be a double portion; instead of dishonor they shall rejoice in their lot; therefore in their land they shall possess a double portion; they shall have everlasting joy." When I look back over my life, I see how God had His hand on me. He wasted nothing. He used every misstep for my good. Be encouraged, Sis, God hears you, and He's right there with you.

About - Tiffany Jones

Called an "A-list performer" and a "rising star" (Philadelphia Daily News), Philadelphia-based vocalist and performer Tiffany Jones has been lauded for the "soul and sincerity behind her voice."

The color of her voice and the melodies of her original compositions are drenched in soul with jazz inflections, while her honest, heartfelt lyrics touch listeners with a message of love, joy, peace, and healing. Tiffany has released two independent recording projects entitled Reincarnation and Him. Her latest single is her first Gospel song entitled "More Than Enough."

Being a wife to her husband, Micah, and a mother to her two daughters, Layla and Morgan, is her favorite job. Tiffany has also worked as a professional vocalist for over 25 years. She holds a B.M. from Temple University and a MAT from The University of the Arts. As a Certified Vocal Health Instructor, Tiffany is the owner of The Jones Voice Institute. She currently serves as an elementary music teacher, a worship leader at Freedom Church Philadelphia, and a session singer for various commercial projects.

IG: Tiffanyjonesmusic

Websites:
TheJVI.com
Tiffanyjonesmusic.com

Deal or No Deal
By Amy Albin

was so nervous. I was so young. I was only 19 when I walked down the aisle on my wedding day to the love of my life. The nerves went away when I saw my soon-to-be husband standing there with tears in his eyes, waiting for me as I walked down the aisle to the song "Every Season" by Nichole Nordeman. I had no idea this song was prophesying my future and to my family. My husband Mark and I have four beautiful daughters who were all born in each season; autumn, winter, spring, and summer. I have always loved children, and my dream was to be a mom. I would always dream of my children, raising them, and the family I would have.

I didn't mind working hard in business or ministry, which was another passion I had in my heart. In fact, I was raised in the ministry, a PK through and through. I didn't dream of a career in business even though I went to college and loved to do big things. My greatest desire was to be a mom and to homeschool my kids during their developmental years. Even more than just a dream, I knew it was my calling to raise them.

Early on in our marriage, Mark worked in construction and became very skilled, so he started his own construction business. Through college, I worked a side job as a secretary in a law firm. It was a good job, and after college, I upped my hours and stayed at the law firm. Mark's business was young and unreliable. It would be good one week and bad the other, and then maybe bad again for a few more weeks while he was juggling bids and jobs. There was never any financial dependability. I didn't make much money at my job but was able to bring a consistent weekly paycheck to put food on the table and gas in our cars. I was thankful for that.

My first daughter, Eva, was born, and I left my job to stay home. During that time, I was concerned about our finances and sometimes wondered how we would make it. A little less than a year later, the law firm called me back and asked me to come back to work. They needed me to do a highly sensitive job that not many people were good at doing, and they offered me a salary for a couple of days of work each week. What a miracle! I could work part-time and make the same amount of money I used to make when I worked longer hours. Because Mark's business was so new and financially rocky, it was a great opportunity for our family. How could I turn that down? So I went back to work.

A couple of months later, I found out I was pregnant with our second daughter, Zoe. Still working my part-time job, now barely making ends meet, I felt more and more like I should be getting a better full-time job to help support us as a family. The family was growing, and so were our bills. For Mark, there was always work and lots of it, so instead of me getting a full-time job, we decided to grow his business. We started to grow by adding several employees and taking on larger and larger projects. As the business grew, all the office work grew too and became harder and harder for Mark to manage on his own, so I became his secretary and also helped him develop his company as well as work at the law firm. Soon to be a mother of two, my heart still longed to be with my kids full time. Even though Mark's job had really good weeks, there still were really bad weeks. I knew this was the season to pray and trust God through these years while he built his business.

Things were looking better in the construction business. It was growing and becoming more stable. We talked about me staying home with the girls. Mark wanted me to. He wanted to care for the girls and me. It looked like I might finally be able to stay home with them after our second daughter was born. Then without warning, the unthinkable happened in Mark's construction business. Mark was building a church several hours away with his construction crew. He had been gone for a long time and was finally headed home for the weekend. His crew was left to adjust one or two of the newly installed trusses to start putting on the roof. It seemed like a simple task after the massive trusses were installed. He got a phone call that something had gone wrong. The wind blew, and the equipment pulled the trusses the wrong way, and ALL the trusses fell and broke off the building! They were completely destroyed! Thank God no one was hurt. I remember that phone call and the feeling of the world crumbling under me. We had to pay for new trusses and cover all the expenses to get the job back up and running. We also had to pay the paychecks to our employees and all the incurred expenses that went along with it. So not only did we not get a paycheck for this entire building project, we had to pay our workers double because of the setback in the time it took to recover the build.

To make matters worse, our insurance company said there was nothing they could do about it. They wouldn't cover the accident financially. Not at all! We fought it but came out empty-handed. We had to bear the weight of the cost of the accident ourselves.

We were in so much debt it felt like we were drowning! We talked about going bankrupt, but we both felt that that wasn't the way to go. We were trapped. The only thing we knew to do was to keep moving forward, trusting God to help us work out the details. Now my dreams of being home with my girls felt impossible. It felt like it would never happen. It felt like every single bill was a roaring lion waiting to eat us as a family, and what little money I had, I would throw it at the bill that was roaring the loudest. Soon I was a mother of two. My heart ached as I went back to work. Thank God for my mom, who watched my toddler and now my newborn. It made the transition a bit easier to handle. I couldn't see through the storm, so I just put my head down and kept pushing forward.

A couple of years later, we were excited to announce our third daughter, Chaya, was on the way! Our oldest was about to start school, and it became harder and harder to leave my young family. I felt more and more torn on the inside. Mark didn't want me to give up on my dream; he wanted me to stay home with the kids after Chaya was born. But how? This was impossible! This was more than impossible. This was foolish! But somehow, I heard the voice of faith in my husband's mouth. He said that he wasn't sure how it would work out, but he just knew it would. I felt trapped. I wanted to trust it was what we were supposed to do, but how could I? Our situation left us financially barren and without hope. Was God speaking, or was it just another hopeless dream? My heart cried as Peter's did in the Bible, "God, if it is you bid me come!"

Thankfully, it was time for our church's women's retreat. This was a time to get away and spend time with other women of faith and be ministered to under the sustained influence of the word of God. To encourage the women, we would write "prophetic encouragements." Let me explain what this is. A number represented each woman. We would pass out those numbers to trusted women of faith who didn't know the name of the woman the number represented, pray over that number and have them write down an encouraging word from God for that woman. For many years we would do this, and many, many testimonies came out of this. I knew this was coming. I was hoping that, by some chance, God would speak to me about my situation. The dream of staying home with my girls but not being financially destroyed, in spite of it, I hoped. Knowing my husband was behind me but feeling as though I needed to hear it straight from the mouth of God, I prayed! How could I walk on water unless I knew it was Him calling me? I would sink if it wasn't Him!

It came to that point of the retreat where we were all handed an envelope with a letter inside. I sat there and opened the envelope, and started reading.

DEAL OR NO DEAL. I, the Lord God, am standing before you, telling you to TAKE THE DEAL! Trust Me, for I am the One who will care for all your needs.

Let me back up a little. Mark and I would often sit down and watch the famous show Deal or No Deal, where the participants would have the opportunity to choose a case that might have one million dollars. The contestant would have a chance to keep the case or have it bought out by the "banker." The host would say "Deal or No Deal," and the contestant would have to choose if they would take the deal that was offered by the banker or not. "TAKE THE DEAL," the very words I had been waiting to hear, the words I could understand. It was Him calling me out of my comfort zone, out of trying to financially support myself, and into His plan for my life! The dream to be home with my girls was His plan for me too! I came home knowing I had heard God's voice. I came home resolved that He would care for the details. I didn't know how or when, but I did know it was Him. Mark agreed with me, and we committed it to the Lord in prayer.

A couple of months later, I left my job when my third daughter was born, never to return. I stepped out of the boat. Shortly after that, the first miracle happened. The debt we owed for the trusses falling was covered, and the bill was PAID IN FULL! In time, the credit card debts that were owed were forgiven and PAID! A third miracle happened, and I don't have answers for how it happened. Mark's pay went from spotty and unreliable to almost triple the weekly pay and never to miss a week again! He didn't even stay at the same job from year to year as we were both on a journey to become servants of the church as pastors, but he never missed a week's pay again! It is a miracle! Twelve years later, I am here to testify to the goodness of God and his favor in our lives! Not only did God lead us into a place of faith, but He led us into a place of peace. I have many more testimonies of how God redeemed our finances and how He led our family from ashes to beauty. I cried out to my Father God in a time of need, and He Heard me!

Four years later, the Lord blessed us with our youngest daughter, Liv, who became the family baby, and brought a lot of love and fun to our family. Now, as I look back and as my girls are getting older, I feel my job as a mom is slowly changing as they grow. I am so grateful that God has given me these years to raise them and invest in the women they are becoming!

Once a woman was asked why she stepped out of ministry to raise her kids. She responded, "Instead of ministering to the hundreds in my ministry, I will minister to the thousands through my children!" Now, as a pastor, I minister to many men and women facing the same fears and the same decisions I once faced, not knowing the future, being scared to step out in faith, and being scared they might fall. I am here as a living testimony to say that if God calls you to overcome your situation with faith, you will not fail, you will not fall, and you will be held in His hands. You can't walk on water, but you can walk on God's Word! Now I see that the song I walked down the aisle to many years ago, Every Season, was testifying that He would sustain me in any season I would walk through! The bottom line....trust Him in every season.

About - Amy Albin

Amy, along with her husband Mark of 18 years, is the lead pastor of United With Christ Church in Johnson City, New York. She serves as a counselor, administrator, preacher, worship leader, and director. She has also assisted in planting several churches through the apostolic network, United with Christ International.

Amy is a soulful singer/songwriter and has written and co-written multiple songs that have been recorded and produced through United With Christ

Worship. She has an apostolic call to the nations and has led worship and ministered at many conferences and events throughout the US and worldwide.

Amy leads with love, uprightness of character, wisdom, and a servant's heart. She is a woman of profound faith who speaks the uncompromising truth of the word with boldness and grace. Her heart is to be a minister of reconciliation to all those she encounters.

Her current focus is pastoring the local church and homeschooling her four daughters: Eva (17), Zoe (15), Chaya (12), and Liv (8), as she directs a thriving Classical Conversations Homeschool Community.

To connect with Amy, follow her on Facebook and Instagram
@Amy.Albin.56 or email her
at Amy.a@unitedwithchrist.org

His Word Sustained Me
By Prudence Shapcott

———⸗⸗⸗———

My head was in a brand new territory, a place with unknown walls and boundaries. Worse still, I felt this overwhelming shadow watching me, following me everywhere and making itself visible only to me. This shadow was definitely not my friend. I was going through the motions of being present with my family and yet desperately trying to process what had just happened to me. How did I get to this place where there was no obvious way back, or how could I undo this thing that had just been done to me? My body did not feel like my own as this dangerously toxic chemical coursed through every fiber of my being. This drug was deemed so dangerous that the nurses doubled up their protective uniforms when administering the treatment. They warned me against even sharing a bathroom with family members for the first 2-3 days after treatment in case a single drop precariously strayed and contaminated someone else with its toxins. "Remember," the kind nurse told me, "this drug is just for you - no one else; you have to flush the toilet twice after each use, wipe everything down, leaving no trace."

Going to sleep on the first night after chemotherapy, I was afraid. Not only was my body exhausted, but I began to experience new strange symptoms. I cried. He heard me. I distinctly heard the Lord's voice break through my thoughts, saying, "Don't be afraid; I am here." It was as if He were literally sitting right there at the edge of my bed. At that moment, everything changed, and I slept like a newborn baby.

During the summer of 2021, I began to notice subtle shifts in my health. Up until then, I had always been in extremely good health and virtually took no medications. My primary health doctor ordered several tests to try and determine what was causing the unusual symptoms I was presenting, but the tests were inconclusive. Finally, she just reminded me to have my annual mammogram. A few weeks later, after a number of further tests and biopsies, I was confronted with the reality of having breast cancer. As a prayer minister and leader of the Joshua Prayer Group (JPG) I regularly pray for people who go through various traumas and teach principles on how to overcome using the word of God and through prayer. I and my JPG co-leaders are so passionate about helping others to experience the power and promises of God that our prayer ministry was named after Joshua in the Old Testament, who led the people of God into the experience of the promises. But now, it was my turn. This was another whole new level challenge for me. How was I to respond? I had entered a place that I had never been to before—physically, emotionally, or spiritually.

Several supportive prayer hubs formed around me quickly, both locally and globally, including my extended family, church, JPG leaders, seminary, and friends from all walks of life. I was overwhelmed by this kind of love; it was humbling to need and receive so much support, both practically and spiritually. How important it is that we allow others to be God's hands and feet and to ask for help or be open to receive it when it's offered. Whether people are offering prayer, food, or other gifts, cheering us along with a word of encouragement, or just sitting beside us during those long chemotherapy sessions, this is how God's kingdom comes, and His healing manifests. The community is blessed and becomes a vehicle for God's blessing. The truth is, this issue is not really about us or our sickness. Rather, God wants to be glorified. This means His vision is always beyond what we can think or imagine asking Him. It's not just you, He wants to bless, but it's anyone you come into contact with, your family, and your community, especially those at the margins. As a matter of fact, one of the simplest ways to pray for healing is to give to the poor. When you give to the poor, God will remember you on your sick bed. See Psalm 41.

One time my entire extended family gathered globally via zoom to pray for me, and on that call, someone prayed for me to have no pain from the surgery. I recall thinking that was a strange request since all surgery involves some pain, right? When surgery finally came, I was filled with a level of peace that I'd never experienced before. I had no fear. The surgeon and the medical staff were amazing. After surgery, I expected the medication to wear off and the pain to kick in, but the pain never came. Weeks later, I reflected on the fact that I did not require even a Tylenol during my recovery from surgery. How grateful I was when I remembered that strange prayer.

If only that was the end of the story. However, a few weeks later, I was shattered to hear that the lab results from the biopsies and tests indicated I needed to have chemotherapy. I wept as I struggled to prepare myself. I asked the Lord, "if it is your will for me to have chemo, then why am I crying?" He answered, "Those who go out weeping, carrying seed to sow, will return with songs of joy, carrying sheaves with them, (Psalm 126: 6). In an instant, the Lord quieted my soul and encouraged me again through His Word.

Sickness is a trial, yet there are blessings in it that cannot be obtained in any other way. My prayer life entered a new dimension. His Presence became so tangible I learned that He really is with us in the valley and in the fire. His Word became sharp, crystal clear like never before. I recalled how one of my seminary professors taught us to always ask why something was written in scripture; what did God want us to know? Applying that basic rubric to all the numerous healing scriptures left me with no doubt that God's will to heal is the default position. For whom are the many promises about healing in the Bible, if not for the children of God? Why did our Lord Jesus receive all those stripes on His body if it were not for our healing? (Isaiah 53:4-5, Matthew 8:14-17, I Peter 2:24). It's His nature to heal, as revealed by His Name, Jehovah Rapha - I am the LORD who heals you (Exodus 15:26) and aptly demonstrated over and over again by our Lord Jesus who healed everyone who asked Him. This God has not changed. He cannot change.

One powerful memory I have from a few days before the surgery was a visit from four African mothers who feed hungry people on the streets every week as part of God's Kitchen Global. We sang songs, danced, and prayed out loud in my basement—what a preparation! They encouraged me to put on the whole armor of God, as found in Ephesians Chapter 6. All the pieces of the armor, like faith, hope (the helmet of salvation), righteousness, and truth, were obvious pieces of armor that I needed. But what the Lord really spoke to me about was that for my protection and healing, I needed to put on my shoes and preach the gospel to myself and not just to others, as I had previously understood this scripture to mean. I needed to remind myself why Jesus died, and these scriptures needed to be in my mouth continually to activate faith. Faith comes by hearing the word of God.

Psalm 103 (NKJV) verses 1-5 became part of my daily meds. And still is.

1 Bless the Lord, O my soul
And all that is within me, bless His holy name!
2 Bless the Lord, O my soul,
And forget not all His benefits:
3 Who forgives all your iniquities,
Who heals all your diseases,

4 Who redeems your life from destruction,
Who crowns you with lovingkindness and tender
mercies,
5 Who satisfies your mouth with good things, So that
your youth is renewed like the eagle's.

I chose to believe each verse literally. So whether I had the mental, physical or emotional energy capacity, I would bless the Lord. Sometimes singing and dancing with all my might, despite an aching body. I rejoiced that God had forgiven me and was healing all my diseases, and had already delivered me from destruction (Ps 103:3-4). Verse 5 became my anchor verse, as I held onto the promise that I wasn't always going to look like this, as the illness had really wracked and aged my body. He would satisfy my mouth with good things: show me what to eat and not eat and renew my youth.

Many don't doubt that God has the power to heal in answer to prayer, but we struggle with the question, "Is He willing to heal me?" I believe the answer is yes since He has no favorites.

Sometimes, there is a direct link between our sins and our sickness. Personally, I found it to be an opportune time to examine myself and repent of anything the Lord showed me. If we say we are without sin, we make God out to be a liar. (1 John 1:10). There is one story in the gospels where Jesus' disciples ask him if a man was blind because of his sin or his parents' sin. The Lord said it wasn't anyone's sin, but it was for the glory of God. I believe every healing is for the glory of God. However, there were other times in the gospels when the Lord made direct links between sin and sickness. For example, after He healed the paralytic man by the pool at Bethesda, He told him to stop sinning, or something worse would happen to him (John 5:14). Therefore, examining ourselves for repentance is a good thing. We always have the assurance that He forgives us (Psalm 103:2, 1 John 1:9).

One of the hardest things to go through in life is when a loved one passes away. But does this change God's perfect will for his people? We don't know all the answers, but the truth is that God is Sovereign and good, yet we do not always experience His will in all aspects of our lives. For example, we know He wants us to love one another in the same way He loves us, but do we do that? He wants all people to be saved, but not all receive Him.

We experience sin, sickness, and death because we are in a fallen world. Neither sin, sickness, nor early untimely death is God's perfect will for us. That's why we need a Savior. That's why Jesus came and as He said, so that we can have an abundant life (John 10:10). That's His perfect will for us. When death comes, it does not mean they or we have failed the test. It is absurd to judge or assume that it was because someone did not have enough faith, but rather, like those who are our examples in scripture, though the loss is always immense, we praise God that it can be said of them:

All these people were still living by faith when they died. They did not receive the things promised; they only saw them and welcomed them from a distance, admitting that they were foreigners and strangers on earth. Hebrews 11: 13 (NIV)

Believing God wants to heal you, believing his word is plan 101 for your battle with sickness. But the most important healing we need is the salvation of our soul because death will come to us all at some point. We should always be ready. We do this by repenting of our sins, surrendering our lives to Jesus, and confessing Him as Lord and Savior. (Romans 10:9-13). He always receives everyone who comes to Him.

The story of how King Hezekiah reacted when he faced death from an illness fascinates me. The prophet Isaiah told him to get his house in order because he was going to die from his illness. Given that Isaiah was a major prophet with a known track record, you would think Hezekiah would accept the message and prepare to die. On the contrary, he pleads his case with God, and the Lord listens and sends Isaiah back to tell him he is going to be ok in 3 days, to go up and worship, and that he will live for 15 more years (2 Kings 20: 1-7).

I say pray for healing if you want to live and plead your cause, no matter what report you receive or from whom. Be cantankerous in your faith in God's goodness and mercy towards you. A New Testament example is the Canaanite woman, who was blocked by the disciples, ignored, and apparently insulted by the

Lord as she pleaded for her daughter to be healed (Matthew 15:21-28). Her daughter was healed. This is the kind of faith that pleases God. Believe Him and His goodness. *Now faith is confidence in what we hope for and assurance about what we do not see. This is what the ancients were commended for. Hebrews 11:1-2 (NIV). Let His Word sustain you.*

About - Prudence Shapcott

Prudence Shapcott is a leader, teacher, and minister of the gospel and is passionate about the Lord Jesus. She is the founder and leader of the Joshua Prayer Group (JPG), an international, ecumenical prayer ministry whose mission is to make God known through the power of prayer.

Additionally, JPG partners with local ministries to serve the marginalized, focusing on providing food for those without and returning citizens.

She leads and speaks at faith-building initiatives such as conferences and women's retreats and has written Bible studies on a number of topics, including social justice.

Prudence and her husband, Lee, serve as Ministers at Freedom Church in Merchantville, New Jersey. Together they teach Biblical Foundations classes, lead prayer ministry and serve as marriage mentors.

Aside from her ministry responsibilities, Prudence is an abstract expressionist artist whose work has appeared in several galleries around NJ. She uses her artwork unabashedly to share her faith. Prior to launching her career as an artist, she enjoyed a successful two-decades-long career in strategic market research and business development in the UK.

She has a master's degree in marketing and product management from Cranfield University, England, and is currently completing her Masters in Divinity at the Reformed Episcopal Seminary, Pennsylvania. New Jersey.

Lee and Prudence have two beautiful daughters.

Contact Prudence through her JPG website: www.joshuaprayer.com or direct email, joshuaprayer1@gmail.com. Watch out for her book *How to Pray the Prayers God Answers Yes*, coming out soon!

From the Pit of Pain to the Place of Purpose
By Ashley Autin

———— ∞∞∞ ————

shley, if you don't stop doing this, I'm going to divorce you." Divorce me? What? He had never said those words before. It had been a bad night. I had found myself, yet again, in a downward spiral. What started out as just a casual drug we used when we danced the night away at raves in New Orleans had suddenly turned into a coping mechanism for me to escape the pain and torment in my mind. Bryce had to come to rescue me, once again, from the casino. I was high on meth and sitting at a video poker machine, just trying to forget the memories. My anger toward God had led me to this self-destructive path, and I did not know how to find my way out. Bryce and I were newlyweds. I should have left behind this life when I moved with him from Baton Rouge. Now, more than ever, I wished momma was here to tell me what to do.

Trauma came into my life at the young age of seven. One day, my baby sister Mildred was playing in the yard while my momma was chopping wood from the haul of lumber my stepdad had dropped off.

Mildred got out of the yard through a gate that had been left open. The cops were called; a manhunt ensued, and my sister's body was found floating in a shallow creek near our home. She was only 18 months old. I would never again see her little smile or hear her laugh or her taps on my bedroom window to wake me up in the mornings. She was gone forever.

After Mildred died, my parent's marriage began to deteriorate. Jerry, my stepdad, began drinking more and more. Parties became an every weekend occurrence at our home. One night during one of those parties, my mom found the courage to leave the man that had abused her for many years and blamed her for my sister's death. She left him for about four months, but after countless threats, she returned home, only to face the hands of her killer. At ten years old, I watched the woman who brought me into this world bleed out from a gunshot wound to the neck and die right before my eyes. I grabbed my sister Brandi and walked in the rain to get help. The next morning, we were told that our trailer had burned down, and we had lost most of our childhood belongings.

Now here I am with my husband, saying he's going to divorce me. How did I get here? This was our first year of marriage. Bryce had just graduated from law school, and we were starting our life together, but I was still stuck in the past. I had left behind my little sister Brandi. I failed her. I was supposed to be the one raising her. I was supposed to be the one protecting her from all the pain that I had gone through. It wasn't supposed to be this way. In the span of two years, I had gotten custody of my sister after charges were brought against our foster parents for sexual abuse.

Brandi had gotten the worst of it. The abuse had been going on since she was four, and I couldn't understand why the God I served would allow such evil to happen to my innocent sister. I tried raising her, but all the trauma we went through just divided us more and more. In our state of complete desperation and not knowing what to do, my friend Lisa offered to take my sister to live with her. Once Brandi was gone, the devil just whispered in my ear more and more. I had come to believe that I was a failure and completely worthless. I was so angry with God. I did not want to feel anymore. I didn't want to feel pain ever again. The meth had turned into an addiction. I would go a few weeks without doing it, and then I would mess up and do it again. I felt like a completely crazy person. Why would I want to continue to use meth?

I had a loving family that had taken me in as their own. Bryce's parents were wonderful to me. They knew I had been struggling with this addiction before we married. I had a complete breakdown in college and had to tell Bryce and his parents the truth to get my life back on track. The last thing I wanted my in-laws to know was that I was still using. No matter how hard I tried, I couldn't stop returning to it. I lived in constant shame. I could never hide the truth from Bryce. I would always tell him when I used. I hated myself for it.

Everything came to a head that night. Bryce had to come and pull me out of the casino and bring me home. He was serious. He had once told me that he would never divorce me. When we took vows, it was for the rest of our lives. I thought he would be the only person who would never leave me, and now I knew I needed to change. I couldn't do this on my own. The last conversation I had with God me telling Him that I didn't need him anymore. I blamed God for everything that happened to me and thought I could handle life on my own. But I could not do this by myself. I went into our bedroom and lay in bed and wept. I cried, and in my desperation, I cried out loud to God, "God, I don't know why you even created me. I don't even want to live anymore. My sister is dead; my momma is dead; Brandi isn't with me; why did you create me? What is my purpose? Please give me something to live for."

About a month later, I was awakened by a deep, loud male voice that simply said, "Ashley." I woke up completely startled and a little scared. I called out to Bryce, thinking he was home, but he wasn't. I hurried, got dressed, and rushed out the door to Golden Motors, where I worked. I felt so strange; something felt off. Then it hit me. I asked my boss if I could be excused. I went straight to CVS to grab a pregnancy test and went to Bryce's office to take it. It was positive! We couldn't believe it. Bryce and I hugged and cried. I went straight to my mother-in-law's house to tell her the news. My body was trembling. I knew now that nothing else mattered anymore. I could no longer live in the past. What happened to Momma, Mildred, or Brandi was not my burden to carry. I couldn't use what happened to them as an excuse to mask the pain anymore. I had a baby growing inside of me.

During my pregnancy, the Father began to slowly strip away the desires that didn't belong there anymore. I cried a lot. I began to recall all the stupid things I did during my addiction...how I hurt Bryce and myself. I called people and began to apologize for some of my behaviors over the past years. My pregnancy was truly a level of healing for me. I was sober. I began to see life through a totally different lens. I started cooking and baking and even tried my hand at painting. There were some funny paintings I did, too. I was happy - really happy. I wasn't numb anymore. I was truly feeling for the first time in my life. I was going to be a mother. My life was no longer in complete moral failure, but God was redeeming me through this pregnancy. I threw myself into my faith and prayed to God to protect my baby from any past mistakes I had made. I gave birth to my beautiful baby boy, August, on Thanksgiving Day. I remember thinking what a good God that I served to gift me with such a blessing on that particular day. I had so much to be thankful for. I was so thankful that the Lord gave me a second chance. He gave me a new life and a new identity. Looking back, I know that the voice that I heard call my name aloud in my bedroom was the audible voice of God. "Fear not, for I am with thee; I have called you by name, and you are mine." Isaiah 43:1

He called me by name. I no longer belonged to a kingdom of darkness but was stepping into the kingdom of light. For many years, people did not know my story of addiction and how I overcame it. I was so fearful that people would label me as another drug addict. That's how the devil works. He keeps you locked up in places of shame, afraid to tell people the real and raw truth about parts of your life. I'm here to tell you that your story could hold the key to unlocking someone else's prison. As I have begun to surrender my life totally to Him, He has just unlocked more and more areas that kept me in bondage. He has closed the doors I had opened to the enemy and has allowed me to walk in total freedom.

I have also found so much freedom in sharing this part of my story. I pray that the person reading this will know there is hope. His name is Jesus. He has never left you - not once. He is your Adonai, your Master. Your ownership belongs to Him alone. The more that you sit in His presence and spend time with Him, the more He will begin to reveal the nature of His heart to you. He loves you more than you could ever fathom or imagine. Even in your darkest hour, in your pit and despair, He orchestrates His beautiful plan to fully give you time to know Him.

Today, as I write this, Bryce and I are happily married, serving the Lord together, and raising our four beautiful children, August, Victor, Preston, and Dianne (named for my momma). My family is my greatest gift from the Father. They are my rescue story. There's a song that Lauren Daigle wrote called "Rescue," and part of the lyrics says, "I will send out an army to find you in the middle of the darkest fight, it's true, I will rescue you." The first time I heard it, the song completely wrecked me. I feel like that song kind of sums up what the Lord has done in my life. He sent an amazing husband to me who saw my heart for the Lord and sent us an army of little children to take care of. Out of our greatest pain is birthed our greatest ministry. These little people are my greatest ministry. I want them to know Jesus so that when they are faced with pain and the troubles of this life that, they know when they cry out to God, He hears them.

About - Ashley Autin

Ashley Autin is no stranger to pain, loss, and trauma. Her story of overcoming great adversity earned her the honor of being selected as a Louisiana Young Hero as well as a Horatio Algier National Scholar. She attended Louisiana State University, where she met her husband, Bryce Autin. Following college, she settled in Cut Off, Louisiana, where she started her family of three boys and a girl. She spent many years of success in mortgage lending, telemarketing, and sales. She and her husband serve at Victory Life Church in Lockport, Louisiana. They teach the children's and youth ministries and serve together on the prayer team. Ashley is also a singer on the worship team. Outside of church, she is a contributing writer to the Christian magazine, Soulful Margins. She has a passion for deliverance ministry and volunteers her time ministering at Lynne's House in Reserve Louisiana, a refuge for broken women. Ashley believes that her primary ministry starts in her home. "When I stand before God, I have to give an account of what I've done with my time here on earth. As a parent of younger children, I stand in the gap for them right now. However, on judgment day, they stand alone before God. I want to leave this earth knowing that I did everything I could to teach them how to have a relationship with Jesus Christ so we can spend eternity together," says Ashley.

Contact Ashley
Facebook: ashley.autin1
Instagram: ashley_autin
Join Ashley's Arise and Shine Group on FB for encouragement about the Lord.

Fasten My Heart
By Erin Hockaday

*"Brethren, I do not count myself to have apprehended;
but one thing I do, forgetting those things which are
behind and reaching forward to those things which are
ahead."*
Philippians 3:13 NKJV

*"I don't depend on my own strength to accomplish this;
however I do have one compelling focus: I forget all of
the past as I fasten my heart to the future instead."*
Philippians 3:13 TPT

"Fasten my heart to the future." That's what I've been doing this year. What an eye-opening experience I've had. In April, my husband and I were exposed to a ministry we had never heard of at a conference in which my husband was a speaker. I listened attentively and then got in the prayer line for impartations. My life has been forever changed. After that night, the Lord opened my eyes to some things deep in my heart. I've had precious times with Him as He has drawn back things He put in me over 20 years ago. The main thing I want to write about is what happened 22 years ago and how it affected me. If I can prevent anyone from doing what I did, then it is definitely worth sharing.

The Lord touched me in a tangible way while I was sitting in Kenneth Hagin's prayer school (led by my husband, Jim Hockaday) many years ago. I suddenly knew I was supposed to have a third baby. Wow, I was excited! Before this moment, I didn't have that desire at all. When I shared this with my husband, he was excited as well. We knew this was God. The Lord impressed upon both of us when it was time to conceive, and we were so thrilled. A series of events took place along the way that encouraged us that we would be having a boy. The part I want to write about is what happened to me. There are two times in my life when I sensed the Lord speaking VERY strongly, and what I thought was VERY clear to me. The first was when he told me I was going to marry my husband, and the second was concerning this baby, that it would be a boy, among other things He shared. So, you can imagine that when I gave birth to our daughter, I was a bit confused. I want to stress how blessed and thrilled we are to have had her! She is wonderful! We love her so much. This is not the point of my story. But instead, how do I go forward with my relationship with God when now I don't know how to hear from Him? (Which is what I thought.) If I missed Him here, then where would I miss Him next? Maybe I just can't hear His voice. Well, I didn't talk about this with anyone. I had a new baby to take care of! That began the next 20 years of me keeping God at arm's length. I had no idea at the time I was doing this. It is just this year that my eyes were open as I wept before God at all the times we've missed together. He wants to be our best friend and help us in every part of life, but He can't do that if we push Him away. He wants to help mothers with supernatural parenting. Wow, did I miss out on that! Don't get me wrong; He helped me in every way He could. My girls were taught the Word and went to church and got born again at a young age, but did they see their mom having a vital intimate relationship with Him? No, because I couldn't trust Him anymore, or so I thought. The devil really blew this one up in my mind! And I swallowed the lie, hook, line, and sinker. But when God opens your eyes to something, how clear it is! I let pride get in. Anyone can misinterpret what they hear from God or put their own thoughts or desires into what He says. We're not perfect, but He is. He's the most loving Heavenly Father!

So, let's talk now about how to trust God with everything in our lives and let Him fix our problems for us. Here's something to think about: Can we get ourselves out of the way? This is a question my husband gives people across the country as we travel and minister. That is the road to freedom in Christianity. We have a magnet that says, "Good morning, this is God. I will be handling all your problems today. I will not need your help. So, have a nice day." I love that! Can we let go and let Him handle our problems? Only we can say if we're in the way of God working in our lives. He wants to work. He wants to do things for us. His Grace is there to do the heavy lifting, to make things easy. He says in His word, "For My yoke is easy, and My burden is light." Matthew 11:30 NKJV We're the ones who make it heavy and difficult. We are the ones who want to be involved. We want to do our part. He says to let go. Let Him do it. It can be hard for us to do that.

A year ago, I had the privilege of going skydiving. That was the most thrilling experience of my life! Because it was a tandem dive, I didn't have to be concerned about any part of it. The man I was strapped to did all the work. All I had to do was follow a few instructions and then just enjoy it. It makes me think of my relationship with God. Because I'm tethered to Him, in union with Him, I don't have to think about anything other than enjoying the ride and the view.

"That they all may be one, as You, Father, are in Me, and I in You; that they also may be one in Us, that the world may believe that You sent Me." John 17:21 NKJV

If we don't know God, we can't fully trust Him, and that's when we try to help Him. But God is absolute. For instance, Jesus said in the gospel of John chapter 10 that His sheep know Him, they hear Him, and they follow Him. Do you see how absolute this is? This is how you experience Him. Believe it, see it, speak it and act like it. He will become real to you. Therefore, we have to be absolute with Him in order to get God's results. The definition of absolute is free or relatively free from mixture: pure. In James, it says, "Just make sure you ask empowered by confident faith without doubting that you will receive. For the ambivalent person believes one minute and doubts the next. Being undecided makes you become like the rough seas driven and tossed by the wind. You're up one minute and tossed down the next." James (Jacob) 1:6 TPT

We can't be up one minute and down the next. Do we want His results? Or do we want things man's way? The next verse says, "When you are half-hearted and wavering it leaves you unstable. Can you really expect to receive anything from the Lord when you're in that condition?" James (Jacob) 1:7-8. TP

With God, there is no plan B, only plan A. So, if we have another plan or two, just in case, then we don't fully trust Him, and therefore we won't get His results. A.W. Tozier said, "Pseudo faith always arranges a way out to serve in case God fails it. Real faith knows only one way and gladly allows itself to be stripped of any second way or makeshift substitutes. For true faith, it is either God or total collapse."

So how do we get to a place of total trust in God, knowing He will perform His word in our lives? Well, how do you trust someone in the natural realm? You spend time with them. You talk with them. You interact with them. You get to know them. They say, "Let's meet for coffee at 10:00," and you meet them, and they're there when they say. You start to believe what they say because, over and over, they follow through. Well, God CANNOT lie. "God is not a man, that He should lie, Nor a son of man, that He should repent. Has He said, and will He not do? Or has He spoken, and will He not make it good?" Numbers 23:19 NKJV

So, prove Him out. See that He keeps His word. Meet with Him, talk with Him, and get to know Him. Not just through reading the Bible but through tangible interaction with him. Proverbs 3:6 says to acknowledge Him in all your ways. The more you invite Him to be a part of everything you do while listening and paying attention to Him, you will have God's experiences. Do this every day. He wants to be part of your life. It won't take long at all until your trust in Him is solid and concrete. In times of turmoil, you have confidence in God because He's your Father, and you've spent time with Him; therefore, you know and trust Him! Then when any situation arises that is contrary to the Word of God, you know it can't last. It must change; perhaps it's not even real! Could your relationship with the Lord be more real than the troubles of life? Get acquainted with the spirit realm because, in reality, it's more real than the natural realm. Take time to relax and get quiet enough to hear Him and feel His presence. We can live in this world and function out of the other world. And boy, is that a fun life! This is the life that I'm learning to live in now that I have let go of the past and the lie that I can't hear His voice. Don't let a past failure of any kind trip you up or keep you from going full-on with God. Again, He wants to walk with you through this life and remove any hindrances in your way. To quote my husband, "Grace is the ability to move the target." That means it doesn't matter how good of an aim you have; you'll always hit the bullseye!

About - Erin Hockaday

Erin Hockaday graduated from Rhema Bible Training Center in 1991 and married her husband, Jim, shortly after. From 1992-1994 she and her husband traveled and sang with the Rhema Singers and Band - the crusade team for Kenneth Hagin Ministries.

The Lord later transitioned their ministry, and her husband, Jim, stepped into overseeing the Prayer and Healing Center at Kenneth Hagin Ministries. During that time, Erin became pregnant with their first daughter. Three daughters later and 25 years, she began traveling once again with her husband nationally and internationally while also assuming the position as Administrative Assistant for Jim Hockaday Ministries. As they travel throughout the US and abroad, they see the miraculous hand of God setting people free, healing the sick, and bringing people into a closer walk with the Lord. Their adventures in God continue to unfold as they have moved from Tulsa, OK, and have started Healing by Design, a healing center in Castle Rock, CO, where they teach and minister to the sick.

Contact info: www.jimhockaday.com

God, I Didn't Sign Up for This
By Tammy Baron

I t's rush hour traffic in a college town near Portland, Oregon. The sound of sirens and the flashing lights of emergency medical vehicles moving to the beat of the clock surround me. Employees were racing to the nearest hospital parking lot exit at the end of their shift. It was a kaleidoscope of people venturing home to engage in their routine lives. This day was busy but no different than most others, as the streets were full of impatient humans honking their car horns. I sat at the stop light, staring into the traffic like I did so many times, thinking of how to create a majestic dinner within a small thirty-minute window. Little did I know this night would become a night unlike any night before. Predictable moments would soon become a thing of my past.

Dinner was a success! I began preparing for tomorrow, hurriedly cleaning up the kitchen. The weekdays were forged with creating memories and topped with sheer exhaustion. After getting the kids off to bed, I finally sat down to watch television. This program was fascinating as they discussed infertility and surrogacy. I had never heard about this innovation in modern medicine. Couples using surrogacy and IVF (invitro-fertilization) technology created a real curiosity within me. Unknown to anyone, I began an adventure to research more about it. Joining surrogacy groups of women who shared their journeys was where I met my friend "Jan."

Jan and I became close friends. She, too, was a working mom, and she had her own personal surrogacy journey. She shared intimate details through the lens of infertility. When I met Jan, she and her husband were awaiting the birth of their baby through surrogacy. Their new baby was going to be a girl, and they would now complete their family of five. Jan was able to answer my questions with such confidence about surrogacy from both her perspective and the perspective of her surrogate.

Time passed, about six months or so, until one day Jan and I were on the phone, and she asked me my thoughts about becoming a surrogate. Jan had said she met a lady year prior through their infertility clinic. Jan was careful to inform me that her friend "Jennifer" had just begun looking for a gestational surrogate as this now was their only hope of having their own child. With eight failed miscarriages and multiple failed IVF attempts, Jan expressed she felt I might be a good fit for them. "I know you and your personality, and I think she will feel at ease knowing you are an experienced mother who does not desire to have more children." It is a common fear that couples face the potential possibility that their surrogate will refuse to give them their baby after birth. I was a good candidate, I reminded Jan, as we both laughed. She could often hear the chaos of my kids at home being kids, and she knew my heart was content with all God had given me. I had no desire to expand my family. Jan encouraged me to think about it. I told her that I would definitely pray about this, talk to my family, and see how they would feel about mom having another baby through surrogacy.

I spoke to my family, attempting to make sure they all understood the unique adventure we were signing up for. The journey would be welcoming a new couple into our lives for the rest of my life. Was I ready for this? Would my family be able to accept all that we would experience with a new pregnancy? The kids were older now; how would they explain this to their friends? Oh, how the questions danced through my head the more real they became in the discussion. As a wife and mom, you want things to continue as "normal" as possible for your family. I must admit that I do not know if any of us really understood the magnitude of the adventure ahead, and yet the vote was unanimous. We were going to help this couple become a family.

I agreed to become a first-time gestational surrogate for this couple. I was only willing to attempt this one time. My unspoken prayer to God was, Lord, if the process works, this will be my personal confirmation to stay on this course. The next few months were a whirlwind of crazy schedules, flights, contracts, lawyers, and an introduction to the doctor who was prepared to make this all happen. Hours of telephone conversations as the biological parents and I were getting to know each other. Next came daily injections of medications, lab visits, and the coordination of care with my local group of providers. I conquered each hurdle with expectation. I felt like a runner leaning in towards the finish line, awaiting to feel the ribbon across my chest to declare, "I made it!"

Three months later, I would fly to meet the couple in the state where the procedure would be done. We will call them Mike and Jennifer. The procedure was successful, and the doctor and I were in the room to discuss my questions. He showed me the ultrasound screen to view where the embryos were placed. I said, "I sure hope this works, Doctor S," and his response changed my life. Dr. S looked at me and said, "What do you mean you hope? It did work, and you will do great." His words echoed in my head as these were the very words of God. In this life, our lips must guard all that we carry in our hearts. One must be intentional and thoughtful before allowing words to be spoken. As I recall, at that moment, God's words shaped the world and formed life. Proverbs 18:21 reminds us that life AND death are in the power of our tongue. I knew God had used Dr. S to set my focus, as we both knew this journey would be a faith walk. That day I was leaving that room carrying a miracle.

Five weeks later, my OB/GYN confirmed I was officially nine weeks pregnant with twins. Nine weeks pregnant, the phone call that I thought would change a couple's life would end up going to voicemail. Days turned into weeks, and finally, a return phone call. I was elated to share this long-awaited moment of joy, but the words I heard changed everything. "Tammy, after much thought, we will not be moving forward with the pregnancy." I was told to abort the pregnancy as they did not want any relationship with them. I was told other things that made me realize the twins and I were now on our own. I couldn't believe what I was hearing! I panicked, and I called my doctor and my attorney to ask for guidance. I didn't want an abortion; I didn't know what to do. A couple of days later, I was sitting in my doctor's office, and he sat with me as I just sobbed. "What do I do?" I recall asking him. He was a quiet, older gentleman and fatherly wisdom seemed to radiate from his countenance. I asked him again, "Dr. B, what do I do?" I didn't agree to abortion. Dr. B sat beside me, and finally, he began to speak.

Tammy, I can't tell you what to do as I am not allowed to do that. I will, however, remind you of what you are. I looked at him, puzzled, and I asked, "What I am?" He asked me again, "Tammy, what are you to these babies?" It was like a rocket launched in my head, and I blurted out, "I am their birth mom. I am their birth mom, right?" He simply nodded and smiled at me. I am a birth mom, and a birth mom in my state has rights. I knew now what I needed to do. I hugged Dr. B so tight that day and said, "Thank you, you have no idea how God used you today to help us three." As I left that office, Dr. B and I knew there would be many more visits ahead.

God will strategically place people in your life to remind you he has not forgotten you. The very situation you are facing may be the ballad in life that ushers people in to discover that Jesus is real.

I set out to adopt two unborn babies. We all signed the agreement relinquishing the parental rights of the biological parents. To this day, I never heard from them again. I was now fourteen weeks along with the twins. Abandoned but not alone became my motto; I recall getting the official document from my attorney stating I was now the twin's legal parent. Jesus, you made this possible, I whispered as I slumped down to the living room floor and began to cry.

Meltdown moments came and went as I cried out, "God, this isn't fair; it's not what I signed up for." This is hard, and it's scary. I don't know what I'm doing. God, you know I prayed about this; I believed you gave me peace. Why did this happen to us? I let myself fall apart and then gathered my composure. These days I would remind myself that we would finish the journey of bringing these babies into this world. God had a plan, and it didn't look like mine, but I knew there was a purpose for it, even if I couldn't see it today.

As the pregnancy continued, I faced some challenges of twin pregnancy—preterm labor at twenty-two weeks. The doctors and nurses were amazed as they did not expect such a positive outcome. The specialist called me to admit me to the hospital at thirty weeks as I was showing signs that the twins could be born any day. Safety first, as the twins were breached, and that would require a C-section. I began running through the realization that I had two babies that I had not planned to keep. I still had no parents for them, nor a couple of interest. The one thing I did have was God. I held my belly in that hospital bed and prayed, "Jesus, please direct me to the right people."

A familiar face peeked into my hospital room. She was a previous work acquaintance. She apologized for coming unannounced but felt a nudge to share with me her family's story—a story of faith, their trust in God, and infertility for seven years. I was moved with intrigue as this seemed too good to be true. After meeting them, it was no surprise I would choose this family to adopt my twins. Quickly, the paperwork would be signed just one month before giving birth to a baby boy and girl. God orchestrated every detail just in time to welcome their children into their lives. In a moment, a family was created, and I gained a wonderful friend in their new mom.

The words in this chapter hold the transparency of one of my life's difficulties. You may be experiencing your own life's difficulty even now. Yet through it all, I need to remind you that God genuinely cares about you. You, too, may look at your life today and find yourself saying, "God, I didn't sign up for this." What I found in my life journey was it was exactly what I signed up for. As God prepares us for what we will face in ways, we may not understand at the time. It wasn't until the adoption of the twins was complete that I recalled a dream I had in March 1989. I had given birth to twins, a boy, and a girl. I realized that God was showing me a glimpse of my future. A journey that would bring many people closer to God. A journey that would help others believe in miracles again.

Never Give Up!

About - Tammy Baron

Tammy and her husband, Sal, are Pastors in Arizona. They have five grown children and have been blessed with 17 grandchildren. Tammy is known for her passionate heart for God's word and genuine love for people. Being raised in the church, she surrounded her life with God's word, and this founded her relationship with Jesus Christ. Tammy is an accomplished vocalist, recording artist, and inspirational speaker. Traveling throughout the West Coast and Canada, ministering to all genres of people, helped shape her view of kingdom destiny along with a near-death experience in 1987. Today this passion continues and has expanded to online broadcasts and guest appearances around the world teaching the good news of Jesus Christ. Tammy has worked in healthcare for over thirty years and believes that this work God has used to nurture a passion within her to reach those who are hurting. Today both Tammy and her husband go to the streets of Phoenix to share the love of Jesus. MARK 16:15 Tammy has a unique gift of using words to capture the essence of God's heart for the people. This chapter is to inspire you and challenge you to ponder the idea that all your life, God has had a plan for you. It's time to walk in your victory and ordained destiny.

2HZGLRY

By Dana Dunlap

---

*L*icense plates are so much fun to decode because there is usually a story behind them. The title of this chapter is my personal license plate on my car. In case you haven't yet deciphered what the title says, let me decode it for you...To His Glory. There is most certainly a story behind this plate, and all I can say is that the reason I am even able to write this chapter and take a breath at this moment is all due to the glory of God! The story behind this plate was a story of God's redemptive love overcoming hatred, unforgiveness, bitterness, self-loathing, and healing through the power of God's active, living Word. Simply put, it was a true valley-to-victory story. It all started on a beautiful spring day on May 18, 2007.

I just glanced at the clock in my mini-van, and it read 3:12 pm. YES! I was on time to pick up my oldest son from elementary school. I parked in my usual spot and was about to get out of the van when my cell phone rang. I didn't recognize the number, but I answered it anyways. I had been waiting to hear back from the surgeon who had, days before, biopsied a lump under my left armpit. I had a little bit of nervousness about the results of the biopsy but really felt overall that I would be ok. When I answered the call, the surgeon asked if I had a moment to talk. I could sense in the tone of his voice this phone call wasn't easy for him to make, and he was a bit hesitant. As he began to talk, his voice got more serious and concerned. He said, "Dana, the biopsy we took from the lump under your armpit is cancerous and aggressive. You will need to contact an oncologist asap to find out how aggressive this cancer is and where it might be located." After hearing the word "cancer," my throat felt like it had dropped into my stomach and my knees and legs went limp. Thank God I was still sitting in my van because that news stole the breath right out of my lungs. The tears began to roll down my face, and fear and panic seized my whole being as I felt I had just been given a death sentence at 37 years old. I kept questioning the surgeon and pleading with him to double-check that it was indeed my results and not mistakenly another patient. It couldn't possibly be mine when I was, for the most part, in good health, and this kind of thing didn't run in my family history. That one phone call not only rocked my world but changed my entire life. My head was swimming with a million questions. My biggest concern was how in the world I was going to share this news with my beloved husband, my kids, and my family. Better yet, how in the world was I going to muster up enough strength to get out of that van, put on a smile and pick up my son from school? This would be the first of many times I cried out to the Lord for His help to just survive in the moment. And this would be the first of many times the Lord heard my cry and answered!

Later that evening, after putting our three and seven-year-old sons to bed, my husband and I finally had some time to process the horrifying news that I was given earlier in the day. As we lay down on our bed, my husband wrapped his strong arms around me tightly, and we just wept for hours. That's all we could do...we had no words. The questions began to swirl around in our heads, and the deadly "what if's" began to take over any logical thinking. "What if" I wouldn't make it? "What if" the cancer is all over? "What if" I can't be a wife to my husband or a momma to my two little boys? We somehow fell asleep that night and were so thankful to put that day behind us.

As the next few days went by, I noticed different emotions beginning to emerge on the scene of my heart. I I felt like I was on an emotional rollercoaster. The magnitude of this diagnosis caused me fear, worry, anger, and doubt in God. I questioned God as to why He was allowing this to happen to me. I wondered what I had done to deserve this. However, a little over a week after receiving the diagnosis, God began to speak to my heart.

One afternoon I can remember crying out to God in utter exhaustion as I lay on the floor with my Bible wide open, hoping that some verse would soothe the wound of my heart. Tears soaked the pages of my Bible as I scrolled through book by book, desperately seeking something to take away the ache. Suddenly, I felt the Lord whisper something to my heart. I heard the words deep in my spirit say, "This is not a physical battle but a spiritual one." What? What did that mean? It certainly seemed like it was going to be a physical battle as I had just learned that the cancer was not only in my entire left breast, but it had spread into my lymph nodes as well. The oncologist had just told me that this type of cancer is aggressive and it would need to be treated aggressively. I would be looking at 16 treatments of chemotherapy, a double mastectomy, and possible radiation to follow. However, as I sat there and pondered what God had just spoken to me, I realized that He was giving me a revelation of the truth about my situation and the key to my healing. At that moment, my heart was filled with confidence that I was going to be ok, but it was going to require some effort on my part. I had a sickening feeling that this wasn't going to be easy, but at the same time, I had a weighty peace fill my heart and a knowing in my spirit that God was for me and not against me. This new revelation of truth was exactly what I needed to be able to stand on my feet and fight. Not just fight this deadly disease but fight the enemy of my soul who was trying to kill, steal and destroy me in my thoughts and body. It was time to take my authority in Christ and stand firm upon the promises of God! It was time to exchange my fear for faith and my tissues for the armor of God.

Weeks went by, and everything felt like a whirlwind of events. My days were filled with scans, X-rays, MRIs, bloodwork, and port placement. Finally, the dreaded chemotherapy began. I wasn't quite sure what to expect physically, but spiritually, I was ready for the battle. God had been showing me in my quiet times with Him specific things that I needed to do to prepare my heart and soul for what was to come. First, God spoke to me about the power of His Word, making its home in my heart. Proverbs 4:20-21 tells us that when we meditate on his Word, it brings health to all our flesh. This led me to search out every healing scripture I could find in God's Word. My husband and I wrote these scriptures on brightly colored posterboard to hang throughout the house. We placed each poster strategically in a place where no matter where we looked, we could see God's promises flood the atmosphere.

Secondly, I was made aware of some spiritual housekeeping that needed to happen within my own heart. Over the years, I experienced deep hurt and rejection from people and situations, which I allowed to turn into bitterness, resentment, and unforgiveness. For the first time in my life, I realized that if I left these three nasty spirits unattended, they would wreak total havoc on my mind, body, and soul. To sweep my spiritual house clean of these things, I was instructed to write a few letters asking for forgiveness, give a few hugs and apologies, and release the hurt to the Lord so He could heal the rest. This was truly supernatural housekeeping. Once I swept my heart clean of these things, I physically felt lighter, like a ton of bricks had been removed from my shoulders, and my mind was no longer crowded with negative thoughts. The Lord had reminded me that just like the aggressive approach that my doctor was using to destroy the disease in my body, God would also aggressively prune, purify, and refine the state of my heart and mind so that I could become everything He had intended me to be. God wanted me to experience His true freedom in my mind, body, and soul. Once I aligned myself with the work of the Great Physician and allowed him to do the necessary heart work, is when I began to see miracles...BIG MIRACLES!

By the fifth chemo treatment, I might have been losing every hair on my body, weighing in at a fragile 98 pounds and feeling weaker physically by the day, but the latest MRI had just revealed that the cancer appeared to be gone! God's promises of healing applied to my life, combined with the spiritual housekeeping, had proved to be the remedy that the Great Physician had ordered. I was witnessing first-hand the faithfulness of God, revealed through my obedience. This was no small miracle, and God gave me this great celebration just in time to help push and motivate me through what would soon be the most challenging part of this battle.

As I neared the last few treatments, God refreshed and comforted my weary soul by sending people to me with strategic heavenly assignments. When there were days I didn't think I could take one more breath or live one more day in tormenting discomfort, I simply cried out His name, Jesus! At that moment, I believed heaven met earth, and God, in his great love and mercy, sent just what I needed when I needed it. Time after time, he would send some sweet angel in the form of a friend who had a hot meal for my family, a housekeeper to clean my house, prayer warriors across the country covering every need, mentors who spoke life into my heart, family members to love on me, watch my kids and do our laundry, a medical professional who prayed with me and chemo nurses who cheered me on with their hugs and encouragement. I saw God answer every prayer as He revealed Himself through so many people. Our God hears every cry and sees every tear. His intention is to always take what the enemy means for harm and destruction and turn it around for our good and His glory. He is a good God who has an open invitation of healing to all people. If God did it for me, He will do it for you!

There were priceless lessons learned through this battle with cancer. God showed me that no matter what we face, He is always present! He is just a cry, a prayer, and a whisper away. He relentlessly pursues us and, through our pain, will reveal His goodness. I realized that this physical battle with cancer was more about the spiritual healing of my heart and exposing those things that kept me from living a free and joyful life. And by the way, God doesn't waste a valley experience! If we are willing, we can take what we have learned in the battles of life and comfort others going through similar situations. Today, I have the great privilege of ministering to women across the globe with the healing and redemptive message of God's Word. He has put a new song of hope in my heart - a song of praise and gratitude for all He has done for me. It was through this battle of cancer that I realized every breath we take here on earth comes from our miraculous God and because of that, my daily life declaration from this point forth has been "It's to His Glory!"

About - Dana Dunlap

Dana Dunlap is a firecracker for Jesus, a cancer conqueror, faith coach, podcaster, and author. She is the founder of the encouragement ministry, "Mind Body Soul Chic." Dana's desire is for every woman to know the healing power of God's Word and be transformed by the redemptive love of Father God. Her mission is to teach women to walk confidently in their identity in Christ and to use their God-given talents to be Trail Blazers for Jesus! She is a speaker for women's groups and has a weekly teaching titled "Spiritual Infusion." Dana lives in the beautiful state of Colorado with her husband and two sons. She loves to thrift shop, interior decorate, journal, drink coffee with her God gals and hike in the Rocky Mountains. Dana's motto is, "Great trials bring GREAT PRAISE!"

My contact info:
Website: www.mindbodysoulchic.com
FB & Instagram: @Mind Body Soul Chic
Podcast: Mind Body Soul Chic on Spotify and the Anchor app

Five Cries
By Melody Behe

I have never had a testimony. When the preacher would say, "How many of you remember the day you gave your life to Jesus and a weight was lifted from you?" Or, "Remember the day you were delivered from this addiction or that disease?" My mind was always blank. I used to joke that I was born saved. But I knew I was supposed to be a part of this book, a compilation of testaments to how God hears and answers the cry of our hearts! It sparked such excitement in me to even be considered, but then when it came time to put my thoughts together on paper, I was blank.

I quickly contacted a friend who knows me well and is a part of this book to tell her I was thinking of backing out! I explained how I didn't know what it was like to be in despair, depressed, or destitute. But then her reply was straight from heaven, and oh, how I recognized the presence of my Jesus in the words she spoke. "Melody," she said. "You have been through more than most people I know!" Then she began to remind me of just how much she had watched me walk through in the 27 years she'd known me, but more importantly, how the goodness of God was so evident in bringing me out without a trace of any of it. There was so much that I had forgotten as it had never happened. I remember feeling like those things were brief moments that were as far from me as the east is from the west. Like stories I had heard about someone else, except the someone else was me! My heart is ever mindful of His goodness in my life, but for the first time, I realized that the real miracle is that He took the turmoil, the pains, and the losses. He removed them from me as if none of it had ever happened!

I'll Not Leave You As Orphans (John 14:18 NIV). These words rang so true in my life like never before after I'd lost my mother. My father passed away 11 years earlier, devastating the whole dynamic of our family. At the time, my internal cry was for my mother. She was so strong, but the sadness I saw in her ran deep. They were both gone by the time I was 30 years old. The feeling of being without both parents was so disorienting to me, like wandering a city whose streets have no name. These were cries that ran deep in my heart. I used to call my mother every Sunday after church and found myself still dialing her number, not realizing she was gone until the automated operator would say, "This number is no longer in service." Then that feeling would begin to rise up again. It took all of me to allow my Heavenly Father to parent me. It sounds strange, but I clung to him as my Savior, whom I loved with all my heart but never really leaned on Him as my Father. I knew He loved me *like* a Father but to accept Him *as* my Father was a newfound trust and assurance! I had been close to a particular family whose daughter I'd considered to be my dearest friend. And so, I began spending more and more time with them. Sunday dinners, basketball games, even tee-peeing houses in the night just for the fun of it. Before I knew it, her parents began to speak into my life as my mother had done. It seemed as though they would be inspired by the Holy Ghost to speak the wisdom of God into my life exactly at the right time without even trying. It took me years to realize that my loving Heavenly Father had not left me as an orphan. My friend's mother would show me how to serve others and how to serve my family. She would show me all the little things in life that young women learn from those that have been there before.

Meanwhile, her dad would periodically speak words of wisdom into my life and eventually walk me down the aisle at my wedding. To this day, this family remains a constant in my life. Not just a good influence but a Godly influence. They are people that cannot be substituted! And I'd like to think that God knew they needed a chocolate daughter!

Advocate, Helper, Strengthener (John 15:16 NIV). Within the same year that my mother passed, a judge granted me a divorce from my then-husband. In a little over two years, we had failed each other with the zealous help of a ministry. Yes, a ministry. Six months earlier, we moved from Tulsa, Oklahoma, to another state to work in a church with ministers that we had seen around Rhema meetings and were briefly acquainted with. Everything seemed good until we unpacked in our new home. We soon discovered that it was a church where everyone was deeply submitted to the Pastor, but no one was submitted to God. I have never felt such a need to escape in all my life. They were in the middle of everything, even our marriage. My husband, at the time, just could not leave. It seemed they had a hold on him that I couldn't understand, but I could only speak for myself. I just couldn't find peace, so I left. Not long after our divorce, I came across an article that told a very disturbing story of how this same Pastor had committed his wife to an asylum against her will, under false pretenses, a lawsuit underway, his arrest for assaulting his teenage daughter, and on and on. Being the variety of spice that I am, I wanted to yell, "I told you so!" But the love of God moved me to pray. The betrayal and sadness his wife and children must've felt, and they had suffered much more than I had! These types of places are designed to grind you down to nothing so that you are completely dependent on them.

I moved back to Tulsa alone. Rebuilding my life was not easy, but I walked with my advocate, my helper, and my strengthener every day as He began to sweep away the debris that this experience had left in my life. He didn't pick up the broken pieces. He made all things NEW. I look back and wonder how I made it. I just kept walking with God. He began to rearrange my heart and mind as I focused on moving forward. It was not easy! My daily decision was to follow Jesus right on out of the shame of a failed marriage. I didn't always feel His presence, but I had a knowing that He was always with me. When I got back to Tulsa, ministers that were like family to me were gracious enough to allow me to move in with them till I got on my feet. They would have prayer meetings from time to time in their home. I didn't realize it at the time, but my Heavenly Father had me there, just sitting in that anointing, allowing it to heal my life. Once I was ready, I broke the news to my sister, who also lived in Tulsa, and moved in with her. Her support was nothing short of a motherly instinct to push me forward. There were times when I knew I could just relax because she was a praying woman. When I was emotionally tired, I allowed her prayers to carry me, so to speak. I am forever grateful.

The Gifts and Callings (Romans 11:29). After being in ministry and having to start life over, I had this looming thought. My internal conversation was, "Lord, what do I do now? Where do I go from here?". I had always served my Lord in some capacity or another. It was not in my nature to go to church, receive everything and give nothing. And so, in my heart, I was crying out for a place to serve Him again. I believe He placed that call in my heart. Soon, I began to attend World Outreach Church. I had been in Pastor Mark and Janet's monthly Holy Ghost meeting for several years straight. I knew what I saw and experienced there was real and from heaven. I needed to experience God like that again! As I grew closer to them, I saw the level of integrity and excellent living in them that erased the mistrust of ministers that was trying to creep in. Their consecration was something I had seen before in Brother Hagin, and I recognized the results of it. I began to serve on the praise team, and it was here that I started to flourish—the fulfillment of doing what He has called me to do dwarfs everything around me. Fellowshipping with Him in that call brings strength to continue on without turmoil. Several years later, I met my now husband and have been building a life with him ever since. We've served side by side in the music department for 13 years now and counting.

Kevin is very laid back at first glance, but he morphs into a Viking warrior when it comes to our son or me! Our friends laugh about it and can hardly believe that he is that way, but God knew I needed someone who would stand up for me! There are so many scenarios that I could go into that require me to call on the Name of Jesus. Losing a job, losing a baby, and on and on. But regulating our mind with the word of God brings strength and growth (2 Timothy 3:16). There is a steadfastness in knowing that the Word of God is alive, living, moving, and rearranging (Hebrews 4:12). We must allow that word to cut through what we feel from what we KNOW. There is victory in Jesus! So today, as I write this, I stand in awe of the practicality of the supernatural. I have no doubt that He not only supernaturally brought me through these things, but He supernaturally removed the effects of them from me! Sometimes with the tangible anointing, but most of the time through consistently following His lead.

To the Ends of the Earth (Act 1:8). Together, my family and I now cry out for the nations of the world. The crisis of life visits everyone. Circumstances rise and fall as the sun rises and sets. They are temporary. But our focus is on life eternal with a loving God. My job, my husband's business, and all the opportunities that come with them are a means to an end. Our focus is to reach past where we are into the eternal. It is the cry of the Spirit that the earth be filled with His glory. This focus will fade out the distractions and detours of decadent self-love that threaten the spread of the gospel. It is the freedom to know that in the big scheme of things, our afflictions are light, as Paul says in 2 Corinthians 4:17. May we never lose sight of eternity with the Living God.

About - Melody Behe

Melody Behe is a 2000 graduate of Rhema Bible College with an emphasis on evangelism. Before and during this time, she volunteered at the Prayer and Healing Center located on Kenneth E Hagin ministries campus for five years. During this time, Melody began to learn and practice the power of praying out God's plan and laying hands on the sick, and seeing them recover. Afterward, she began serving in ministry in various capacities putting into practice what she had learned in Bible college, such as being led by the Spirit of God and walking by faith. Melody currently serves at her home church on the worship team at World Outreach Church of Tulsa, OK, alongside her husband, who is the bass player. As the church's name implies, world missions are a major focus of what God has called it to be, and this vision was planted deeply into her by her Pastors, Mark and Janet Brazee. Professionally, Melody is an accountant at a public wealth management and accounting firm. As a wife and mother, Melody enjoys traveling with her husband, Kevin, and her son Maximus Alexander. Together they support world missions through several ministries.

It Takes Courage
By Valarie Smith

—⌒⟡⟡⌒—

"Be of good courage,
And He shall strengthen your heart,
All you who hope in the Lord."
Psalms 31:24 NKJV

There is a bit of nostalgia as I write this story. One of my favorite poems is "The Road Not Taken" by Robert Frost. Throughout life, I have found myself at many proverbial forks in the road. On the surface, I was faced with the frivolous decisions of youth, like which activities to be involved in, which clothes to wear, and who to be friends with. But underneath a facade of high achievement, I was aware of the secrets I had to hide. I had lived through a series of sexual molestation and abuse. With a strong longing to belong, my moral compass broke as I made choices that I thought would take me on a journey of happiness. However, it only took me on a reckless path to remorse. The roads we choose all lead somewhere, and as Frost writes,

"Yet knowing how way leads on to way,
I doubted if I should ever come back."

As my misguided behaviors created more traumas and remorse, the pressure of the facade grew into striving for perfection and unrealistic expectations. I was searching for acceptance in any way I could get it. One path of experimenting with drugs, drinking, and men. Another path of high marks, leadership roles, and being there for others. Trying to walk these two opposing ways of life created a toxic cycle for coping and eventually led to burnout.

This moment was just before my senior year of college. I was disgruntled with life and felt lost, and I wasn't really sure where God was. Being raised Catholic but not attending confession since 8th grade, I wasn't too sure I wanted to talk with a priest. During this time, I lost a friend to a drunk driver, grieved a lot over the life I had been living, and cried myself to sleep. My best friend was in a toxic relationship. I was afraid for her well-being but didn't have the emotional capacity to respond. The mornings were hard and met abruptly with facing these realities and trying to move past where I had been. Somewhere in that fall semester, I began talking with God. It began with telling God what I was thankful for each day. I shared with Him that I was frustrated and angry with what had happened in my short 21 years. I talked. He listened. And that Thanksgiving, I made a promise to God; the next man I would have sex with would be my husband. It was a new beginning for me, in a way. I had no idea what I was doing, but I knew what I had been doing was not working. I was going to focus on my studies, keep my head down, and walk the path to graduation.

I continued to talk with God through Christmas and the winter months. I asked hard questions about what happened to me in my childhood. The pain from that experience is what led me to explore the power I could have over my own sexuality and use that with men. But that led me to such heartbreak and hurt. I knew I didn't want a man in my life. If things changed, it would be up to God. My best friend was walking through the grief and recovery from ending the toxic relationship. Every night we would share three things we were thankful for with God and each other. I wasn't completely better, but I was being real.

One night a couple of my sorority sisters ran up to my room from the basement and urged me to help with the Airband. This is a competition during spring week where choreographed dance is set to a montage of music. It is high energy, fun, and kind of ridiculous. They needed one more girl because the fraternity had an extra guy in their group than what was originally planned. I reluctantly agreed and followed them downstairs. They walked me over to the group in the cleared living and dining area where they were rehearsing and introduced me to my partner. His first words to me after we were introduced were, "I become submissive around women." To which I responded, "Then we will get along just fine." We laughed. As the weeks of rehearsal went on, we spent breaks chatting together. He was likable, and I quickly learned we had some similarities and were looking for the same things for our future. There was no pressure for anything romantic since he had a girlfriend. Our conversations helped me heal even more. Then he told me he had broken up with his girlfriend. We spent one night together just before I graduated. Then I missed my period. I figured it was the stress of wrapping up school. It was just late. But it didn't come, so I took a test. I was pregnant. Just when life seemed to be healing, I found myself at another fork in the road. I found myself pondering for a flash what the path would be if I were to abort my baby. It would be a quiet and discreet solution. As quickly as that thought flashed, I jerked to reality, knowing what road I would take.

Deciding the next steps together, we told our parents we were pregnant and worked through the disappointment from them. We married three months later. His senior year at university was not what he thought it was going to be, and I certainly hadn't planned on marrying and having a baby, derailing the road I had mapped for a career. I was back in the town I was hoping to leave after graduating, feeling remorse yet again. I spent time questioning what road I was on. One day I remembered the vow I had made. The next man I slept with would be the one I married. Remembering that didn't bring any relief.

After our son was born, things didn't get any better. There was frustration, disappointment, regret, and each day the feelings piled higher. We decided to move across the country so my husband could pursue a graduate degree. Admittedly we also needed space between our families and friends in order to give this marriage a real chance. This took me down a whole new road. Unfortunately, moving away only increased the tension as our circumstances felt even less controlled. My husband reached his breaking point and called out to God, by whom I felt abandoned. Things started turning around for him, but I felt left behind and like God wasn't listening to me at all. We decided together to start going to church. Shortly after, my husband also started attending a local bible school to keep himself growing, and his rededication set me on edge. I was frustrated that he was not going to be home two nights a week. The tension grew between my husband and me; however, in reality, the tension was between God and me. I was so frustrated with this road of life and it not being what I thought it would be. It had potholes and speed bumps, and the only exit ramp that I was able to see was divorce. Knowing in my heart that the exit would not lead to anything resulting in happiness, I felt like I was stuck.

As the weeks went by, I watched my husband live differently. He was more peaceful. He was more attentive. He was more patient. It was downright irritating. As the end of the Bible school classes was nearing, my husband invited me to attend a service, and I quickly responded with excuses as to why that was not a good idea. Our son was barely old enough to go into the nursery, I worked full-time, and we were already going to a church. Why would we attend a service at a different church? With such love and understanding, he met my concerns with compassion.

As that service approached, my husband communicated that he understood I didn't want to attend, and he respected my reasonings and decision. I was confused. Why would he want to go to another service after being in classes on Mondays and Tuesdays and attending a different church on Sundays with our son and me? What was it about this teacher that he wanted to visit? I was not about to let him go to the service without me, so I joined him. I went, knowing our son would not go into the nursery. I went, expecting to have to spend the time in whatever area they had for a parent with a clingy 15-month-old. I went because I didn't want him to go any further in whatever his journey was without me. I went because there had to be another option besides divorce.

Walking through the doors into the foyer, I held my clingy son. After being at work all day, there was no way I was going to be able to get him to go into the nursery. I was directed to a dimly lit room with rockers and gliders, a one-way window into the sanctuary, and a speaker set at a comfortable volume to hear the service. My husband asked if I wanted him to sit in the room with our son, and I could be in the service, but our son was not having that option. I thanked him and told him we would be fine. I made myself comfortable as worship music gently filled the room. My son fell asleep in my arms as worship time was wrapping up, and I settled us into a rocking chair for the duration of the service. This moment of time was like a cocoon of peace. I rocked and listened to a message about God, the Loving Father, that touched my heart so deeply. He loved us so much. He did not leave us as orphans to figure out life on our own, but from the beginning of time has always wanted to be in a relationship with us – with ME! The weaving of the thread of the redemptive plan of God from Genesis to the monumental moment of Jesus' death, burial, and resurrection was so that we would never have to live life and experience hurts separated from God. As the words were being poured out from the speaker's mouth, my whole body tingled, starting at my feet and rising to the top of my head. I was sure my hair looked like a balloon had rubbed it and created a static charge making it stand on end—even though it didn't really. I saw moments of my life, the ones that I had hidden away in the depths of my heart, flash through my mind. I saw Jesus there with me in those moments.

Hurting when I was hurting. Loving me when I felt unlovable. And then I heard these words "He loved us so much that He sent the Holy Spirit to dwell in us and come upon us to empower us to live a new life." I wasn't sure what it all meant, but I knew it was another fork in the road. Having the power to live differently was what I needed. I knew the path from this moment forward was not going to be perfect, but it would be new. I was scared, but I stood up in the cry room, sobbing to the Lord, and walked courageously to the one-way window to pray with everyone that was praying at the altar in the sanctuary. He heard me. He had always heard me, even when I didn't know or understand. It takes courage to keep walking. It takes courage to make mistakes. It takes courage to get up and try again. It takes courage to surrender to a new road.

I have spent many years walking this new road, and I have grown. I have tripped, and I have felt stuck at times, but the feeling of remorse no longer hangs over me. That feeling left that night in the cry room where I cried, He heard, and my son slept. Now I have an ongoing sense of peace. When the morning comes, I ask God for the courage to face the day and whatever comes my way, and He strengthens my heart. I share about the different roads I have walked and the ones I now walk with God with anyone I believe will benefit from them. Knowing the Holy Spirit empowers me each day and helps me to be a better person, spouse, and parent. I have faced loss, cancer, more loss, lack, and rejection. I have found relief from remorse and the courage to stand for what I value. This road that I have ended up on, as Frost writes in closing his poem, "I took the one less traveled by, And that has made all the difference." This new road has made all the difference.

About - Valarie Smith

Valarie Smith is the Administrator and Co-Lead Pastor at FCFTucson, a life/ministry coach with FCF Int'l, a mother to three amazing adult children, and gets to do life and ministry with her best friend and husband, John. She helps oversee and administrate the local church and is part of God's work of resuscitating lives in Tucson, AZ, and beyond.

Before the calling to Co-Lead Pastor in 2019, Valarie served for 15 years with FCFTucson in various capacities, including family ministries, administration, teaching in the church's bible school, hosting girl's retreats, missions work, and teaching at the jail and homeless outreach/recovery centers. She has a BA in Spanish with a concentration in International Business and is also a graduate of Faith Ministry Training Institute.

Valarie enjoys spending time with her family, traveling, running, gardening, and drinking good coffee with friends, and she is continuing work toward a Master's Degree.

Connect with Valarie
Facebook/Instagram Valarie.Smith.35
Email: valariesmithauthor@gmail.com

But God...
By Arcie Brown

I grew up in a great Christian home. I was loved by my Daddy, Moma, and my two sisters and one brother. Our parents took us to church every time the doors were opened. God was big in our home, and I am so thankful that we lived our Christian faith during the week and not just on Sundays. I was saved as a teen and had a real heart for God and Church. My Daddy and Moma always encouraged me to be all I could be. They would say, "Arcie Ann, you can do anything you set your mind to do."

I think I've always been a happy girl. Moma said when I was little, people would ask, "Does she smile all the time?" I tend to have the "Pollyanna" approach to life. "If you look for the good, you will find it," even in the hard times.

As I said, I was raised in a Christian home, but I was divorced by 22 – not good. I thought I'd never be able to serve God again. I felt like I had a neon "divorced" sign stamped on my forehead, and I would never be the same. I knew that I loved God with everything in me, but because of the hurt and rejection, I backslid, which was something I thought I'd never do.

Several times in my twenties, I would go to church, backslide. Go to church, backslide. You get the picture. I was still loving God and honestly miserable. It seemed like the divorce had left me wounded, insecure, and defensive. When anything seemed like rejection, I would immediately go into defensive mode.

Before I got married, I had what I call a "check in my spirit." I loved him – but something in me never felt good enough. I was very active in my church. He started coming with me but decided after marriage that it was not for him, and I did not know any other life than the church. Because of our differences, it did not work. I think I knew inside but did not know how to follow what God was telling me.

BUT GOD...

He continued to work in my life and heal me. That's one thing that I have in my heart is to teach and help young people to know God but also to know how to listen to the inside as the Spirit of God will guide you and protect you, leading you into the abundant life that Jesus has provided for you. I remember in my hurt from the divorce crying out to God and saying: "God, I am so hurt, my heart is crushed, and I will never be the same."

BUT GOD...

Several years later, in a church service (so thankful for the local church) – the minister said, "There is someone in this service which has said, 'My heart is crushed, and I will never be the same.' God is going to heal you today." And then the healing of my broken heart began. I love God! He is so good and so faithful – even in our hurting and painful times – He is faithful to heal us. I believe the corporate anointing in church services will heal us when we also have our hearts open to hearing God. At 30 years old, I went to a Spirit-filled church and rededicated my life to the Lord for the last time. I was home.

I got married again and, two years later, packed up everything and went to Bible school. Moving halfway across the country to Tulsa, OK, was a big thing for me. We went to Rhema Bible Training Center, Kenneth Hagin Ministries, which was in 1984, and I graduated in 1986. It was an amazing time. I loved every class. I am so thankful for my Rhema Family and the Word of Faith teaching. After graduation, I moved to MI and worked in a church up there for four years. I met some wonderful people who are still great friends.

In 1991, we co-founded Life Fellowship Church (LFC) in Bowling Green, KY, and later, the Redeeming Love Church in Gamaliel, KY. Our church went through some things, and in 2001, I became the Senior Pastor of LFC and was ordained through Kenneth Hagin Ministries. A group of people and I stayed together: God has been very good to the church and me. It has been an honor and a privilege to serve the Lord and the people God has brought to our church family.

As I became the Pastor of LFC, God and I had some real heart-to-heart talks. Like, He told me to "hold the church together." I said to Him, "God, I'll do what you tell me to do, BUT YOU will have to do this. I do not know how, BUT I will follow your lead." His next instructions to me, "Get it going again." With that, God dropped a new vision in my heart for the church: Life Fellowship Church, where the voice cries, "prepare ye the way of the Lord..." Bringing people from darkness to LIGHT.

I love that even in our darkest of times, God will give – <u>fresh vision</u>! – and <u>new hope</u>!

I would look in the mirror every day and say: "Life is good, and my future is bright!" Did it look like it? No! Did it feel like it? No! But every day, I would continue to say that.

It took a while, probably about a year. The sun was shining on this Spring day. I looked out my kitchen window, and yellow daffodils were blooming in my yard. I took a breath and said: "Life IS GOOD, and MY FUTURE IS BRIGHT!" And – I knew it was true. Sometimes we have to walk things out. Stay steady – don't let go – don't quit – KEEP WALKING with GOD. I tell people sometimes, just keep walking, and you'll walk right into your bright future.

He IS bigger than any problems. He IS brighter than any darkness.

I have always loved to sing. Music is a big part of my life! As we see in **Isaiah 54:1**, there is power in song. I know that songs can either build us up or tear us down. I have always loved to sing and worship God. I remember once having a special song that someone in my life had given me. After he was no longer in my life,

I would play that song over and over and over again and cry and cry. It was not a pretty picture. I was tormenting myself. One day, when I was doing this, the Lord said to me to "stop it." He said YOU are an "emotional cutter." I knew immediately what He was saying to me; I was just repeating the pain and not healing. I obeyed God, stopped it, and healed.

I had never heard the term "emotional cutter," but that makes sense. God wants to heal us and see us live happy and prosperous lives. Thank God for the "power of a song" as when you sing God-songs, He will lift you up and turn you around.

In 2016, I knew that something was going on in my body. And I knew it was NOT good. I can tell you there is nothing like staying in the Word when disaster hits. There is an enemy out there; his job description is to "kill, steal and destroy," and he's good at his job. BUT GOD... is greater!

I was vacuuming the sanctuary at the church the Saturday before I was going for my doctor's appointment on Tuesday. As I was talking to God, I heard Him say in my heart: "Little girl, you're going to be okay. Eyes on Me." I went straight to one of my friends and told her, "Get ready; next week, we are going to go through something. But the Lord already told me, "I am going to be okay! Eyes on Jesus."

I went in for my doctor's appointment, and they found a blockage in my colon. The doctor immediately got me in with a surgeon the next day. Can I just say here that when you go through something, who you surround yourself with is important. You want family and friends who are Word-talking, faith-filled pray-ers to surround you and stand with you. I had natural family and spiritual family standing in faith with me.

The report from the surgeon was that I did have something. It was moving up and down my colon, into my intestines, and back down again. He even said he didn't know if he could find it to get it out. He was a Christian doctor, and I told him, "You can do this." He did. When he walked into my room after surgery on Thursday, he said, "You are a weirdo. In my 28 years of surgery, I have never seen anything like that." It was Stage 2 cancer - encapsulated – moving up and down. But, I had been in the Word concerning healing, and I would say over and over that, I was healed, and whole and that cancer could NOT attach itself to my body! And it did not! Now my confession is that it cannot live in my body!

"The Word of God is Life to us and Health to ALL OUR FLESH." **Proverbs 4:20-22**. I am so thankful for God's faithfulness in fulfilling His Word in our lives. Jesus died so that we can have abundant life." **John 10:10.**

I remember another time when "one word from God" touched my heart and turned me around. It was at a ladies' meeting. I had gotten discouraged and thought that I could not continue on and that maybe I should just quit. At a ladies' meeting they used the scripture: **John 4:34.** "Jesus saith unto them, My meat is to do the will of Him that sent Me, and to finish His work." BOY – did that scripture hit my heart. What will keep me going is to DO HIS WILL and finish HIS

WORK! It's NOT about me! It's about HIM and finishing His plan for my life and the Church that He has set me over. And on we went. You have probably figured out by now: I love the church. I believe that the local and universal churches were put on the earth with great purpose. Have I been hurt in the church: who hasn't been? Have I been disappointed in people who call themselves Christians but do not live what the Word of God teaches? Oh yes, who hasn't been? But I know that people, even the closest to us, will unintentionally hurt us.

That's why the Word tells us to know each other by the Spirit and not the flesh. And I like to say it this way: to know the heart of the person. Every one of us has said something or done something that we wished we could immediately take back or undo! Amen? Let's start extending the same grace to others that we would like extended to us.

Back to my story: "Many are the afflictions of the righteous BUT the Lord delivers us out of them all." **Psalm 34:19.** "I cried unto the Lord, and He heard me..."

BUT GOD...

The Lord has healed and restored ALL. Nothing is too hard for God. Even in the lonely times, He is ever present to be with us and to fill all those empty places. He replaces hopelessness with hope. Hurt with healing. Sickness with health. He restores all with no evidence of damage. He's just good like that. He is good and faithful. "He never leaves us nor forsakes us."

The Word of God is very real to me. It is forever settled in Heaven, never returns void, and God will hasten His Word to perform it! My prayer is that people would come to know God, and allow Him to heal them so they can enjoy the abundant life that has been provided for them through Christ Jesus.

"I cried and He heard me..."

About - Arcie Brown

Pastor Arcie was raised in a Christian home and saved in her teens. She was a successful hairdresser for 15 years after high school before going to Rhema Bible College from 1984 to 1986. In 1991, she became a Co-Founder of Life Fellowship Church in Bowling Green, KY, and later Co-founded Redeeming Love Church of Gamaliel Kentucky.

She became the Senior Pastor of Life Fellowship Church in 2001 and was ordained through Kenneth

Hagin Ministries. The Vision God dropped in her Spirit for the church was:

"Where the VOICE cries, prepare ye the way of the Lord, Bringing people from darkness to LIGHT."

She has a love for the local church as well as a mission for all people being changed by the power of God, a heart for all generations to worship and grow together to build the church. Arcie has ministered on the mission field in The Netherlands and in Guatemala, as well as in churches and ladies' meetings stateside. She believes that even in the hard times, God is still good and faithful. His love never fails, and He will be with us always.

According to Jeremiah 29:11. He has good plans for each of us: "They are plans for good and not for disaster, to give you a future and a hope."

Areseebme2@aol.com

Father God: The Compass of Great Parenting
By Dr. Pamela Henkel

Finding My North

*L*ike so many women, I dreamed of white picket fences, unfailing whimsical love, and having the ideal family as a reflection of God's goodness on my life. I would learn quickly, through disillusioned eyes and gut-wrenching disappointment, that sometimes God's goodness comes packaged in what he *doesn't* allow. My journey in parenting started with a loss. The loss of innocence I felt as a bright-eyed youthful woman married to an agnostic inebriant; The loss of joy I experienced when I realized that the life growing within my newfound pregnant body wasn't, in fact, welcomed by my life partner and that awareness then succumbing to the actual miscarriage of my first child, and the ultimate ending of my first marriage.
But God.

"God sets the lonely in families"- Psalm 68:6
Devastation would be my friend for a little while as God gently prepared my newly converted understanding to meet His will head-on. It would be His hand of mercy

that cradled me through such loss. I remember the prayers I had for my husband to change and for us to have a family, and with one unimaginable blow to the heart, all of it went up in flames. With grace and grief, I mourned those losses. I took counsel from a ministerial mentor whose words were like angelic balm to my wounds. "Borrow my belief in who you are until you can believe in yourself again," he'd say. Those words would carry me through the darkness of my healing process, changing my life forever. Time under the tutelage of God and my faith brought me great solace, and with time, I was able to live, learn, and love again.

God's goodness met my life in the form of a man named James (whom I affectionately call Jay). We fell in love, got married, and naturally willed to start a family. This time, biology would be the culprit, and I was once again faced with the threat of loss. My body was unable to carry out pregnancy on natural terms, and Jay and I were faced with the decision of medical remedy or the option of adoption. After seeking the counsel of the Lord, I felt that adoption was best.

When the Compass Takes Over
Like any other faith-filled couple, my husband and I sought the Lord. We received prayer from our congregational leadership and prophetic utterings concerning the way we would conceive. We held onto our faith, sought the Lord, and eventually surrendered to His navigation.

"For my thoughts are not your thoughts, neither are your ways my ways," declares the LORD. "As

the heavens are higher than the earth, so are my ways higher than your ways and my thoughts than your thoughts."
Isaiah 55: 8-9

His navigation would lead us to His providence, His providence into prayer, and prayer into parenting. God was about to prove doubt, divorce, and shame a liar, and Jay and I; our lives were about to change forever.

One day, Jay and I received an invitation to minister at an inner-city church. Per usual, we were also invited to fellowship afterward and stayed around to pray for people. It was then that I met the most precious little girl, who was known as the "alter girl," carrying around anointing oil to give to ministers as they prayed for people. After witnessing us pray for others, she waited until the end and came up to us requesting prayer. If her adorableness at four years old wouldn't be enough, her prayer request gripped my soul beyond understanding and displayed the magnitude of God in a tangible manner. Her big brown eyes met mine, and I knelt to her request.

"What do you want Jesus to do for you, dear heart," I said. "I want a mommy," she uttered.

As imagined, every tear constructed in my body met my eyes, and I prayed for this little soul to have a mother—such a bold request. So innocent, and yet, so near.

Not long after, I noticed the alter girl accompanied by an older woman who had one other small child. We ended up speaking to her and found out that she was the great-grandmother of Alice, the alter girl, and her precious little brother named Jordan, who I instantly fell in love with. She, too, had been praying for parents for the little ones, as she had been taking care of them full-time. As faith and fate would have it, she became family in every way; a great-grandmother to our children, a maternal figure to me, and a lifelong prayer partner. We saw the hand of God orchestrating something bigger than we'd imagined. Jay and I became witnesses of His goodness and the new adoptive parents of both Alice and Jordan.

The Compass of Life Begins

We received Alice and Jordan with open arms and open hearts, as the Lord willed. We signed our adoption papers with the respect of communion, sealing the parental responsibility both naturally and spiritually in awe of what God had done. We instantly became family, and the Lord showed His favor through their addition to our home.

"Adoptive mothers give birth too, just through the heart"- Dr. Pamela Henkel

Jay and I were the new proud parents of two children. We prayed for a while, remaining faithful in ministry. We would not long after begin to receive prophetic words about having more children, twins to be exact. In the years to come, God would show His favor yet again, and Jay and I were about to see the miraculous hit our lives like never before.

We received our third child and second son, Colton. God had prepared my heart by showing me in a vision a little boy running towards me, calling me "mommy." It brought pure joy to my heart. Colton had been taught through experience that life was not easy. We prayed for God to help him unlearn that lie. Then at the age of 4, he cried out from his stroller with joy, "I have a family." It was obvious that God was healing my little boy's heart. One year after that, we were blessed with yet two more miracles; our twins, Ana, at 27 weeks old, and Jayson, at 24 weeks old. Surely the Lord had increased and blessed us, but it didn't come without a fight. Once again, the threat of loss knocked at my door, but this time, I knocked back. Ana and Jayson were both born prematurely. However, Ana and Jayson had life-altering ailments, including a possible loss of hearing and sight, along with the unforeseeable backlashes from suffering from withdrawals. The hospital staff advised us that there was a strong possibility of invalidity in Jayson, deeming him a possible cripple and thought not to survive. Doctors advised that if he did live, he would remain a victim of several life-altering handicaps, including hearing impairment, for the rest of his life. We were told that Ana wouldn't be able to walk on her own and would need braces for her legs.

But God.

The "mamma bear" in me rose to the occasion. I was no longer a grieving, doubtful, young bride. I was now a spirit-filled, assured, anointed wife and mother of five children, reluctant to receive faithless word pronounced over God-ordained children. I took the matter to the Lord in prayer and to the doctors in faith. I told them to remove the breathing tube from my son's throat and the bag aiding his breathing.

Miraculously he began to breathe on his own. By the tender age of three, we watched the Lord heal and restore him to complete health, despite the recommendation of medical staff.

Similarly, I watched the hand of God heal my little Ana's legs at three as she requested to run under the healing power and authority of the God I served. I had seen Him do too much. He had shown me His faithfulness; by faith, He established and kept my growing family.

Shortly after, we would meet the hand of God again through our relationship with our children's great-grandmother and receive yet another blessing; a daughter named Rosie. She was brought forth through a prophetic dream had by her great-grandmother- of two girls holding hands running through a church. That next Sunday, Rosie came to visit and held hands with my other daughter, and they began running through the sanctuary. The Holy Spirit quickened me to remember the vision, and I knew then; Rosie would be the final addition to our family.

Checking Your Compass
"For I know the plans I have for you, declares the Lord,
plans to prosper you and not to harm you, plans to
give you a hope and a future." — Jeremiah 29:11
My journey started bleak and void of shape, like a journey without a compass. The irony of God and His goodness is that it unravels in the mystery of trust, obedience, and perseverance against all odds. Suppose I had given up after losing a husband and a child and

mourning a life outside His will. Suppose I had chosen an agency instead of praying for a small child at an altar. Suppose I lost faith when prophecy didn't meet biology in my womb but instead met my faith and sprung forth double portion. Where would I be? The short answer is without my promise; more than that, I would've never gotten to know God as my personal compass. I would've never found the overwhelming solace of His sovereignty in my life and His compassion to meet my needs and desires when I committed to aligning my will with His way.

I want to encourage you today to invite Him in. It is my hope that my journey has inspired you to welcome God into your personal journey. That you were able to pull faith from my story and know that if he could move the mountains of opposition out of my way, how much more He is invested in doing the same for you. Our problems are no match for His plan. Our pain is no match for His providence.

If you ever find yourself in the belly of the wilds of life and find yourself looking for hope in your navigation, remember my story and know that God is your father and an even greater compass in your journey.

About - Dr. Pamela Henkel

Individuals seasoned with generous amounts of charisma, compassion, and undeniable essence possess the kind of ingenuity that shifts the world into its own greatness. Stewarding these traits in an unyielding measure is the spirited professional Dr. Pamela Henkel. Dr. Pamela Henkel is an International best-selling author, multifaceted compere, speaker, elite coach, CEO, and Founder of both Purpose with Pamela and Pamela Henkel Ministries. Her multifaceted production and International radio conglomerate fashioned to enthuse women, entrepreneurs, authors, and diverse professionals to take hold of their life's purpose. Dr. Pamela Henkel's mission is to add value to as many lives as possible by reminding them that they are here on purpose with a Purpose by Design and not by default. Partnering her passions with sincere regard for higher learning, community, and achievement, Dr. Pamela Henkel's career remains a reflection of creative grace, captivating the hearts and minds of many. She holds a doctorate in philosophy, Christian leadership, and business. Living life as one dedicated to the service of people and hosting a myriad of professional skill sets without compromising her dedication to humanity, Dr. Henkel has maintained a nonpareil presence in the modern business world. As the creative founder of Purpose TV, The Pamela Show, and more, she extends her podcast, International radio, and social platforms to promote the voices of many on a global scale. Her propensity for success in her field has led her to award-winning achievements, such as the nomination as one of the Top 50 Women of Business, an elite membership of the Power Voice, and personal mentorship from a world-renowned speaker and mentor, Les Brown. Dr. Henkel's trusted expertise has yielded her various leadership positions, such as Client Enrichment Program Director at the Million in You Lifestyle and Head Coach for the Inner Circle. Dr. Pamela Henkel calls Minnesota home, where she is wife, mother, and grandmother to her loving family. She always encourages people to be the salt and the light everywhere they go. Dr. Pamela Henkel. Leader. Energizer. Philanthropist.

https://linktr.ee/Purposewithpamela

Whose Report Will You Believe?
By Jami Luzecky

"Who has believed our report? And to whom has the arm of the Lord been revealed?"
Isaiah 53:1 NKJV

Growing up in a single-parent home was not easy. My mom was required to work full-time, and my sister and I spent many of our days with a babysitter. I have fond memories of us rolling down grassy hills, playing outdoors, and making up silly games. However, in those early years, I never knew what the day would bring, and that didn't really matter to me. Life was on a schedule, so I did what I was required to do. We frequently moved; and I therefore attended many different schools before I was a freshman in high school. Inevitably, at times I dealt with insecurity and loneliness. As I entered my twenties, I had no clue what direction my life was going and that is when I decided to take charge. I enrolled in college and became an avid planner. Suddenly enthused with my future, I mapped out the next ten years. I was obsessed with plotting every step. I began this planning later than most, but that didn't stop me from dreaming big. The thing I knew for sure was that I wanted a family of my own.

My planning included taking a few mission trips which led me to attending Bible School, and then desiring to be in full-time ministry. There I found the love of my life, and we were married a few years after my graduation from Bible School. We lived in Ohio during the first year of marriage, surrounded by family and friends, and we were also heavily involved in ministry in a local church. The next step, the step that I felt would obviously complete our lives, was to have babies. My plans were interrupted when we moved back to Oklahoma, where my husband began traveling full-time with a ministry team. This move was a difficult time for me as I felt like I was going back in time. I had already been there for Bible School, found my husband, and was now ready to move on; I specifically wanted us to do some kind of ministry together. I believed I had been called to five-fold ministry, but during this phase of my life, I stayed home while my husband traveled. At times I felt frustrated that my husband was traveling and doing what I thought we were going to do together in ministry, but I was "stuck at home." I left my family, my friends, and my church for this?

During this difficult time, as I was reading God's Word, this beautiful scripture seemed to come alive for me—Matthew19:29 - "*And everyone who has given up houses or brothers or sisters or father or mother or children or property, for my sake, will receive a hundred times as much in return and will inherit eternal life.*" This made sense! I decided to take God at His Word and believe it for myself.

As soon as I shook off the disappointment, it became clear there were many goals I had yet to accomplish. I finished my degree in Sociology and graduated Cum Laude in 1993. I was back on track! I was more than ready for the next step in our lives, babies! I yearned to have children and create a loving family. My husband's job did not offer insurance, and neither did mine, so we had to wait. I was frustrated; my timeline was off again.

A few months later after my "timeline realization," Bill and I attended a church service in my hometown. Dear friends of ours, who had no idea what I was going through, spoke godly words of encouragement and life to me which softened my heart and— I was flooded with peace and realization that we were in the right place and going the right direction.

After college, I thought I was ready to step into full-time ministry, but that door still had not opened. Instead, I started a new job with amazing insurance and benefits (praise God!), and it was finally time to have my baby! After a few unsuccessful attempts, I became anxious. Family members and friends were getting pregnant, and I wondered if something was wrong with me. I was 30 years old, so maybe I was too old to conceive. I read some inspiring books (one being *Supernatural Childbirth* by Jackie Maize) and began speaking God's Word over my body. In April of 1995, I took a pregnancy test, and it was positive! To say I was elated is an understatement. I called everyone to share the wonderful news before I even had my first doctor's appointment. Bill and I were standing on the Word and believing for a perfect pregnancy.

Late one night, while my husband was in Canada with the ministry team, I started to bleed. Fear gripped my heart, so I called Bill on the phone. After he prayed with me, I had peace. The next morning, the hospital's ultrasound discovered no heartbeat in the baby. My heart broke. My doctor assured me it was normal to miscarry during the first pregnancy.

I was not informed of this baby's gender, but I felt in my heart it was a girl and had already picked out a name for her. On June 2nd, 1995, I had a D&C. It was one of the hardest things I had ever experienced.

Shortly after, I started planning my second pregnancy—three months later, to be exact. My obsession with this detail caused a little stress between my husband and me. I wanted to be right on schedule. In October of 1995, I was pregnant again! My husband was on the road, so I flew out to Las Vegas, Nevada, and surprised him with the miraculous news.

During one of Kenneth E. Hagin's meetings, Brother Hagin walked over to where I was seated and asked me to stand. He did not do this very often, so I was nervous and unsure of what to expect. He laid his hands on my head and said, "The Lord will restore unto you that which is lost, have no fear; the blessings are near!" He didn't know that I was pregnant, but I knew that Word was from God. I wrote in my journal that night: *This baby will LIVE and not die and will declare the works of the Lord*. I had no idea how tightly I would need to hold on to those powerful words.

Because of my last pregnancy and my age, my doctor suggested scheduling a few extra ultrasounds to watch the progress of the baby. Every ultrasound looked good. In January of 1996, at four months pregnant, an ultrasound revealed our baby GIRL. We were so excited! I quickly began decorating her room—pink everything.

A few days later, I received a phone call at work, and my doctor asked if I was sitting down. My heart raced. He said the most recent ultrasound spotted something on my baby and that she would not live to be normal or healthy. He "assured" me of the "normalcy" of this because of my age and that another pregnancy could be totally fine. He suggested I come in right away to terminate the pregnancy and start fresh. I burst into tears at the thought of losing another baby, and I was furious at my doctor's suggestion.

Not even five minutes later, my dear friend pulled me into an office and prayed fervently over my baby and me. I was determined, no matter what the report, this baby would live and not die, and she would declare the works of the LORD! *I Cried, and He Heard Me!*

I immediately switched to a Christian doctor who believed with us that our baby would come into this world healed and whole. More ultrasounds confirmed the potential issues, but we all stood strong on the Word of God: "Have no fear, the blessings of God are near." We knew that God's blessings were good and perfect, never imperfect. *Every good and perfect gift is from above, coming down from the Father of the heavenly lights, who does not change like shifting shadows."* (James 1:17).

More and more negative reports came our way, but we knew that God's report trumped them all. Bill and I started singing a song that we both had known for years: "Whose report will you believe? We will believe the report of the Lord!" Every time fear crept in (which was often, let me tell you), we would sing that song:" Whose report will you believe? We will believe the report of the LORD!" The lyrics go on to say (and we inserted "our baby"), "His report says our baby is healed; His report says our baby is whole; His report says our baby is free; His report says VICTORY!" We would speak God's Word that this baby was healthy and whole from the top of her head to the soles of her feet.

In February, I experienced horrible pains in my side. "WHOSE report will you believe? We will believe the report of the Lord!"

In April, her heartbeat was way too high. "WHOSE report will you believe? We will believe the report of the Lord!"

One night while I was laying in bed, I could not feel her moving at all. "WHOSE report will you believe? We will believe the report of the Lord!"

Just a few days after my due date, in the wee hours of the morning, contractions began. I had peace in my spirit, but in the back of my mind, the worry for her health lingered. Throughout the hours of labor, we either sang or spoke the Word of God over our baby.

All day long. That evening, our doctor held her in the air and said," She is perfect!"

Natalia Anne Luzecky was born, and God's promises were true, just as we believed. Natalia's name means "birth of the Lord." She was our miracle baby! And better yet, God gifted us with a wonderful detail: her birth date was June 2nd, 1996, exactly one year after her sibling went to Heaven. What a mighty God we serve!

For weeks after her birth, I held her and walked the perimeter of the house, singing, "You deserve the glory and the honor, Lord; we lift our hands in worship. For you are great, You do miracles so great, There is no one else like you."

A year and a half later, as I was pregnant with my son Nicolas, Natalia had a fever that led to a seizure. *I Cried, and He Heard Me*. Almost instantly, fear gripped my husband and me. We learned this was a febrile seizure and would probably not happen again but to watch closely if she were to have any more fevers. The enemy loved to use that against me, and I would panic almost every time she got a fever. We took her to the hospital many times for little things, and she was always fine!

Terminating this pregnancy was never an option for us, so the enemy tried for years to take her life. Random symptoms and accidents proved that, but God remained faithful to His Word.

To this day, we don't know if God performed a creative miracle while she was in my womb or if those reports from the doctor were untrue. Either way, we serve a BIG God whose report ALWAYS trumps man's Word. HIS report is the one we choose to believe. We serve a God who watches over His Word to perform it in our lives! We serve a God whose gifts are ALWAYS good; He is a GOOD, GOOD FATHER.

Today, not only is Natalia being used mightily for the kingdom of God, but my son Nicolas is also. They are BOTH anointed worship leaders working in full-time ministry. They are extremely gifted and intelligent and love God with their whole hearts. They both have already touched many lives in their 26 and 24 years on this earth. While the enemy tried to wipe out our precious gift from God, GOD was in the works, providing us with DOUBLE. Nothing can stop Him!

Many wonderful, godly people lifted our arms, rallied with us, and prayed over us. One scripture that was spoken–I will never forget–was James 1:17.

"Every good and perfect gift is from above, coming down from the Father of the heavenly lights, who does not change like shifting shadows, and perfect gift is from above. God's gifts are perfect and good, and He is incapable of imperfection."

About - Jami Luzecky

Jami was born in St. Petersburg, Florida, and grew up in Dayton, Ohio. At 19, she traveled to Israel, seeing parts of the countryside where her Savior lived and walked! Her heart was full, desiring to reach the lost. As she journeyed to several other countries, her passion deepened to reach those who didn't know the Lord.

Jami attended Rhema Bible Training Center in Oklahoma, receiving her Bible Degree in Missions. She married Bill Luzecky in 1991, a fellow Rhema graduate, and they moved to her hometown, Dayton. While teaching at a Christian school there, she also realized a deep love for children's ministry, so she began pursuing a degree in Education.

Moving back to Tulsa, Bill traveled with Rhema Singers & Band as Jami taught kindergarten at a Christian Development Center and graduated with her bachelor's degree in Sociology.

After the births of their two children, Natalia, and Nicolas, they relocated to Canton, Ohio, where Bill joined Faith Family Church as an Associate Pastor. He continues to serve as a Family Care Pastor to this day.

Jami dedicated her life to developing her own children, actively ministering to other young people, plus counseling and encouraging women from all walks of life. She leads various Connect Groups and coaches Connect Group Leaders at her church.

In 2016, she co-founded "Not For Sale; One Step At A Time," an organization dedicated to providing awareness and preventing human trafficking. Yearly, Jami and the NFS team host a Walk for Freedom in North Canton with multitudes participating.

While working the past 12 years at a local real estate office as the office administrator, she enjoys quality time with her family, photography, and travel; she looks forward to all that God has next for her life.

The Promise Of Barren Tears
By Deanna Freeman

What do you do when the answered prayer is the source of your tears? How do you handle it when the promise causes you to question, "Was it really worth it?" Who do you turn to when the tears of expectation turn into tears of discomfort and distress? You mimic the words of the Psalmist David and say, "You've kept track of all my wanderings and my weeping. You've stored my many tears in your bottle - not one will be lost. For they are all recorded in your book of remembrance." Psalms 56:8 T.P.T.

All I've ever wanted was to be a mother. All I've ever wanted was to have a husband and many children, six to be exact. If mothering were a major in college, it would have been mine. All my hopes, dreams, and desires hinged on being a mother to many, six to be exact. See, I am one of two children; therefore, six seemed like many to me. Fast forward to 1997, I fell in love with the man God chose to love me through, and in 1999, we married. We do what many do next. We immediately begin our journey to parenthood.

Year 1...nothing. Year 2...nothing but tears. Testing, diagnostic surgeries...more tears. Year 3...

tears; years 4, 5, and 6...screaming, kicking, and more tears! How could this be? I cried so many tears that at some point in time, there was no sound because I began to feel guilty for crying so much. I thought, who wants to always see me crying over the same thing? But don't you worry, the Father doesn't mind your tears. I believe in the power of prayer. I believe in the power of faith. I believe in miracles. I would immerse myself in the Word not because I wanted this from God but because I really love God. I would attend service after service, women's retreat after women's retreat, Bible study after Bible study, prayer meeting after prayer meeting, always encouraged that my God would deliver! In every encounter with the people of God, I wanted them, or better yet, I needed them, to agree with me in prayer that my husband and I would have children.

After two failed IVF cycles and borrowing money to pay for those cycles, we had nothing but tears to show for them. That is until one retreat in Myrtle Beach, S.C. The Spirit of God was tangible! The power of God was present, and I remember crying out in silent screams like Hannah.

"God! Why would you put this desire in me? I just want to be a mom!"

Hear those words, "I just want to be a mom." Not birth a child but *be* a mom. At that moment, I felt the overwhelming peace of God like never before. A calm reassurance from The Father that He had heard my plea, that no request had gone unheard. But here's the thing, I know He heard me, but I recognized it wasn't until my desire aligned with His desire for my life that peace occurred. It didn't happen until I aligned my will with His will for my life. It didn't happen until what He wanted for me took precedence over what I wanted for myself. He reminded me that my mouth had always been praying to birth a child, but my heart just wanted to be a mom!

Aren't you glad that He knows our heart's desire? It wasn't until I took the limits off the limitless God and allowed Him to operate in ways I couldn't even fathom. When I released God to really be Lord in every area of my life and said, "How you do it doesn't matter," He did it!

Now let me be clear, motherhood didn't happen right away, but at that moment, there was a promise that had become connected to my tears. These tears now came flanked by the promise of God that I would be a mother to many. These tears came with the awareness that He not only heard me but that He also did exactly what He said He would do. Hallelujah!

In 2006, we adopted our first son. In 2009 we adopted our second son, and in 2010, our first daughter. The miracle of our children's adoption stories can't fit into this chapter but know that He worked miracles through them and their birth mothers as well. I have never been filled with as much joy as I was at that moment. Was everything perfect? Absolutely not. However, everything that was promised was given. Or, so I thought.

Now let me just be clear, this chapter is not about our infertility journey. It is about standing on

God's promise while tears stream down your cheeks. It is about having your tears shift from joyful to painful and back to joy again. It is about being in a place where walking out the promise of God sustains you even while it brings discomfort and distress. It is about knowing that when you cry, not only does He hear, but He is faithful to respond. And respond is exactly what He did!

Let's fast forward to March 2016. My husband is called to interview for a position that would cause us to leave North Carolina after 17 years and head to N.J. As he is preparing for the interview, I am asked to accompany him. What! No, I don't need to go. I may mess it all up! Of course, I obliged and found myself in a classroom at our home church, classroom Number 9, to be exact. This classroom was a place I had called on God so many times. This was a place I had cried most of my tears. This was the place where people stood in agreement with me for what my heart desired. My husband and I are in this classroom with four people who traveled from New Jersey to conduct the interview, and one young lady asks me something along the lines of, "How do you handle stressful situations?"

Honestly, I had been through a lot in my life, some things that, for all intents and purposes, should have taken me out, but they didn't really shake me.

My response to her was, "It's life!"

Question after question, I gave the same response, "It's life."

See, I firmly believe you deal with life and move on. You take what you've been given and make it work.

I really do believe "all things work together for the good of them who love God and are the called according to His purpose." Roman 8:28. Nothing really bothered me. That is until Wednesday, April 27, 2016.

On that Wednesday, I received a call from a social worker in N.J. that two of my nieces and nephew would be removed from their home. They had previously visited us in North Carolina, and I informed the social worker that if anything had ever happened, I did not want them in the foster care system. He remembered our conversation and called as a courtesy. My husband and I talked briefly and agreed that we would intervene. Thursday, April 28, I travel alone to N.J. and go straight to the courthouse, where upon completing the paperwork, I am informed that there is a family court date already scheduled for the following day. Friday, I show up for court, and this mom of three walks out of the courtroom as the mom to three and legal guardian of three more. We travel back to N.C. for a week, then all head to N.J.

The Freemans are now temporarily a family of eight, temporarily being the key word. Here is why I believe God has a sense of humor. Remember, in March, hubby interviews and is selected for the position. April, we get the call about the children. On May 6, we closed on our home purchased for five as a family of eight. But no need to worry. This is all temporary (insert the laughter of God).

2017- family of eight; 2018 - family of eight; 2019 - family of eight, and here we are as you read this book, still a family of eight.

Oh my, here come the tears again!

If you recall, previously, I stated that all I wanted was to be "a mom to many children - six to be exact." I now find myself with six children, all around the same age. Believe me, all who knew my prayer request served as frequent reminders of what I had prayed about for years.

So, why am I still crying? Why are these tears not tears of joy? When and why did these tears shift to tears of discomfort and distress? Why does this answered prayer hurt so much? Because along with the promises of God comes the process that He uses to mature us. Promises don't come without a process, and often time it's the process that shakes us. It is the process that causes us to flinch. It is the process that hurts. This process of kinship care that God used to fulfill the promise for me to be "a mom to many children - six to be exact" has taken me to the limits of what I thought I was capable of handling. I can only "look to the Lord and His strength; seek His face always." I Chronicles 16:11

Here is what I have learned, and I pray it finds you and helps you. Both the promise and the process of God is to serve one purpose, and that is to bring you closer to Him. As you walk out His will for your life, you will have times of pain, times of sorrow, and times when it may not make sense. Still, thanks be to God that "His grace is sufficient for us and His strength is made perfect in weakness" II Corinthians 12:9. I appreciate that He knows the desires of our hearts and uses them to bring us closer to Him. The bonus to strengthening our relationship with the Father is that He gives us what we ask and uses that for His glory. My tears are just starting to shift after almost seven years of being a "mom to many - six to be exact." My barren tears came flanked with the promise of God, and even now, I continue to rejoice. My prayer for you is that you stand firm in knowing that your tears are not in vain. Know that your tears are strengthening you as they fall. Tears of the righteous are our heart song. Rejoice in knowing that when you cry, He hears you.

About - Deanna Freeman

Lady Deanna Freeman is an anointed and powerful motivator and teacher. She is an intercessor with a passion for embracing the lost, empowering the least, and enhancing the lives of women.

Lady D currently holds a Bachelor of Theology from North Carolina Theological Seminary but is always seeking knowledge to enhance her life and the lives of those with whom she has the pleasure of connecting. She was licensed to preach the Gospel in October 2008 and was ordained in June 2013.

Lady D counts it an honor to be married to Bishop Clifton E. Freeman Jr since May 1, 1999 and is blessed to serve alongside him at Mount Calvary Missionary Baptist Church in Camden, NJ. There she serves as the lead for their women's ministry: B.L.A.Z.E (Beautiful Ladies: Anointed, Zealous & Expectant), as well as fellowship director. She hosts a weekly women's prayer call and also facilitates a monthly women's bible study.

Lady D has the joyous privilege of guarding the hearts of & homeschooling their three children: Joshua, Jonathan, and Aubry, plus 2 of her nieces and nephew- Angel, Christina, and Ziheim. Her children hold her presence hostage, so, at any time, you may find her "momming" on the football field, the basketball court, the track, or cheerleading competitions around the state. She would have it no other way!

Lady D is a sought-after preacher whose most earnest desire is to see the Body of Christ walk in their God-given freedom. This desire is the catalyst for her founding Living In Liberty Ministries Inc (L.I.L.) in 2011. L.I.L. Ministries focuses on reminding believers that we are not saved to live bound, but we have been "MADE FREE & BORN FREE to LIVE FREE & BE FREE in J.E.S.U.S.!"

Lady D would love for you to connect with her via email at FirstLadyD@MCMBC.net.

Follow her on Instagram @LadyD_Freeman and @Cleanwithsimplicity to learn how to enhance your life by living a more chemical-free lifestyle.

Faith on Auto-Pilot

By Stefani Havel

rowing up in a faith-based home, believing in God was just what we did; it was life as I knew it. I attended private catholic schools. Our family attended church weekly, and daily prayers were said around our family dinner table. We were intentional about serving others, giving to those in need, and tithing consistently to our church. On November 8, 1987, my life was forever changed. Life as I knew it would never be the same.

I was in my third year of college at the University of Minnesota Duluth. I was a co-captain on the University Dance team and pursued a major in public relations and communications. I had a solid three-year relationship with my boyfriend, who was a rising star on the college hockey team. Life as I knew it was good, and even though I was living away from home, I kept my faith-based practices of weekly worship and daily prayers. It was just something I did and came without much thought.

On this sub-zero cold and snowy Sunday, I was focused on studying for my first trimester finals and ready to meet up with friends for a study group. Having spent the night at a friend's house, I decided to go back to my house that Sunday morning to pick up some papers and items to bring to the study group. I was scurrying around, getting ready to leave my house and back to meet my friends on campus, when I heard a knock at my door. As I opened the door, there was a police officer in full uniform standing there with a note in hand. He asked to speak with Stefani Havel. I quickly responded that it was me, and I began to ramble that yes, my car was parked outside, and I knew that I was in a no-parking zone and parked on the wrong side of the street. I pleaded with him that I was only parked there for a brief moment, and I was getting ready to head back to campus.

I also sweetly reminded him that I was a poor college student and couldn't afford a parking ticket right now, and I promised to move my car in a few minutes. He gently raised his hand and said, "Ok. That's not actually why I am here, Stefani. We received a phone call from your father, Rudy, and he has been trying to get a hold of you, but your phone/landline has been busy for the past 30 minutes. He asked us to find you and have him call him right away. I thought oh geez. This is so like my Dad, checking up on me to be sure I am studying for my final exams and see to it that I was feeling prepared for my final exams. I asked my roommate to end her conversation, so I could use the house phone to call my Dad. At his first hello, I cheerfully began to ramble, "Hi, Pops! I'm sorry you couldn't get through the line. I'm on my way back to campus to study and feel prepared for finals, so there is no need to call in the police!" As my father began to speak, his voice was audibly shaken, and he could barely speak the words I was about to hear that forever changed my life. Stefi, in a crackling voice, mama died today. Your Mom died today.

Wait. What? You mean Grandma. Grandma died today? No honey. Your Momma, Caroline, died today.

I listened in shock and disbelief. What? How? Why? At the young age of 48, my mother died in her sleep. She had been battling cancer, but she was getting better. I had just spent the weekend at home with her last month, talked to her on the phone on Friday night, and read all her weekly letters, telling me stories of shopping with grandma, working at her hair salon, and the latest family drama. This stuff doesn't happen to people like me, not to my family. We were Christ's followers and faithful children of God.

There was silence on the phone. I dropped to my knees in shock and disbelief. I could hear the stoic whimpers of my Dad on the other end of the line as he told me my brother was going to make the three hour drive up to my college to pick me up and bring me home.

I was devastated. Angry, sad, mad, and heartbroken. How could God do this to me? To my family and most especially my Mom? She did everything right. She attended church worship every week, lived a servant life, prayed daily for others, and so generously tithed. How can you take a life from a faithful "child" from a faithful family?

Everything that I thought or knew about God, having faith, no longer seemed real and didn't seem to matter. Life as I knew it would never be the same.

I felt so lost and hopeless. I was a 19-year-old college student with no Mom. Who was going to help me through life challenges? Who would I tell my "boy" troubles to? Who will I be able to confide in when I need advice on the drama that consumes a 19-year-old college student?

After a week of mourning, funeral proceedings, and a lot of MN hotdish, we all moved forward and adjusted to our new normal. As it does, life went on. The sun would rise, and the sun would set every day. We continued on with our lives, and I resumed my everyday faith with hesitation. I decided to leave the University, the dance team, my boyfriend, and my friends and be at home with my Dad and siblings. It was a strong, stable, loving home for us, and I felt comfortable.

As time went on, I began to feel adjusted and moved on with life in my career, family, and friends. I was making wedding arrangements to marry my college sweetheart, the star hockey player. I finally felt life was getting back on track, and life as I knew it was good. Or so I thought. Eight years later, I was at home with my father on a beautiful spring Sunday evening. I was again scurrying around my house, making final wedding arrangements, planning to move out of Minnesota with my fiancé, and starting our new life together in Nevada, where he planned to further his hockey career. I had quit my job and took up working at a temp agency so I could plan my wedding, get ready for my move to my new home and secure a new job. It was that Sunday night that would forever change my life again. My fiancée, living abroad playing professional hockey, came home earlier than expected. I was thrilled. He was home one month early and would be able to help me finalize our wedding plans and pack for our new adventure in Las Vegas, Nevada.

Unfortunately, he had other plans. A lot of other plans that didn't include me. He sat me down at our kitchen table and proceeded to tell me that while he did love me, he was not ready to get married and move out to Nevada with me. He stated that he still had plans to move to Nevada and pursue his hockey career, but not with me. The wedding was off. The relationship was over. He was moving on without me.

In one moment, he decided the direction of my life. This was not my plan.

I felt so lost, alone and hopeless. Life as I knew it had no meaning. I didn't have a Mom to share in life and laughter. My boyfriend of nine years no longer wanted to marry me. I had no job and no career planned. My Dad had met his new wife and sold our childhood home, so I would no longer have a place to live. No job. No house. No boyfriend. No Mom.

Where is this all-loving God that I was raised to believe existed? When are God's life blessings that I grew up believing would happen to begin to pour into my life? I did everything right. I was a faithful child. Why do these terrible things keep happening to me?

Why would God put desires on my heart to be married, have children, a successful career, and all of HIS blessings and give me nothing? What is the point in believing in a supposed all-loving Father, praying, and serving others if nothing was happening for me?

As I progressed through life without my Mom and without a husband, I was learning that God was not rejecting me; he was redirecting me. He wanted me; He needed me to change my life flight pattern.

I came to understand that God was always working for me. He is always working for you. When it's not the direction we want to go, when we are feeling rejected, we need to take his redirection. We must be open and ready to receive the goodness He sends through, not letting circumstances, situations, or people define our life direction

God will give you turbulence to get your attention. Sometimes it's to help us realize we need to fly a different path to avoid the hurt and pain or give us the strength to press on and weather the storm.

I have overcome challenges, had to break through limiting self-beliefs, and surrendered to the acceptance of the life God has planned for me. The life he redirected for me. Our lives are not always going to go according to our plans. Often times they will go in the opposite direction. The desires in your heart may not always be fulfilled. However, It's in the darkness when you need to look to the light and find the ways that GOD is redirecting you. Let go of the circumstances that you think define you. Leave the people who are not willing to put on a seatbelt and ride through the turbulence with you.

Learn to live a life and love life with God as your pilot.

About - Stefani Havel

As an Ambassador of Affirmations, I teach others a unique mindset system that helps transform thinking and breakthrough limiting self-beliefs. It is a system that works to help you take action, overcome self-doubt and enable a change within you to enrich your life and ignite your passions.

If you desire to live a Level 10 Life, you need to start each day believing you are a Level 10 person. If you want a better life, you need to learn to be better. This starts with FLY, which means to First Love Yourself.

Stefani has presented her Affirmations story and taught over 3,000 people across the country about her unique mindset system. Her Facebook group is growing to over 500 members, where people share their name affirmation.

As a certified DiSC trainer from the Wiley Institute, Stefani helps teach & mentor others on understanding behavior styles so they can best understand themselves and communicate with others more effectively. She has helped coach & train employees across Fortune 500 companies to use this method to communicate with peers and management both professionally and personally.

As a top-producing Branch Sales Manager, I specialize in recruiting high-performing Mortgage Consultants and coaching them forward to achieve peak performance, financial success, and personal satisfaction. As a sales expert, I have the proven ability to maximize sales in a highly competitive market and am a dynamic leader and team builder who consistently motivates others toward success.

In 2011, I was selected as the Loan Officer of the Year by the Minnesota Mortgage Association. I was the 1st recipient of this ongoing award given to originators who are outstanding and excel in loan origination, customer service, and community outreach.

In 2021, I achieved Wells Fargo Leaders Club status, ranking #19 of 223 managers in Distributed Home Mortgage. Entry to this elite group of managers across the country is earned by achieving top rankings across seven categories in productivity, loyalty, and employee retention.

She can be reached at 612-940-7335
or Sparklotta711@gmail.com @Stefihavel

Free From Anxiety
By Diane Hoffman

I grew up in a loving and wonderful home. I can remember always being very shy, timid, and afraid of many things. My family never attended a church which left me with very little knowledge of the love of God or the power of His Word. Without the light of God's Word, darkness can take control, and you see the worse possible outcome in life.

I met my husband selling cars, as we both worked for the same dealership. I was on the new car side, and he was on the used car side. He had been to RHEMA Bible Training Center, which I had never heard of, and said he had a call of God on his life and had to follow that call. Not knowing what any of that really meant, I just knew to say YES to it all. One of the best decisions I have ever made.

I had never lived away from my family, but I just knew we needed to go. I wanted to help my husband fulfill the call of God on His life. We moved from Indiana to Virginia in 1992. The church was located in the country, had a very small congregation, and we lived in a home they rented for us. The home was set way out on 135 acres. It was so beautiful. My son was three when we moved, and the hardest part was taking the only grandchild at that time so far away from my family.

After about a year, I began to have these major panic attacks. I had no idea what was happening to me. My life was happy, the church was growing, and things were going well. One day I was fine, and then it seemed like I was paralyzed by fear the next day. My heart would race so fast it felt like it was going to explode. Nothing I did would make it stop. It began to control my life. I couldn't be around crowds, I didn't want to be alone without my husband, and I could not even drive my car. I felt like my world was spiraling out of control around me, and I didn't know how to gain control again. I thought I was going to die or end up in a hospital. It seemed like there was no way out, and it was a very dark time in my life. I felt trapped and didn't know a way out.

Six months probably went by, and I felt like I was drowning with nobody to save me. My husband couldn't understand what was happening, and I didn't know how to explain it. I just know that this anxiety was taking my life and destroying my life.

Months of tears and being homebound because I was scared to drive my car anywhere felt horrible. I was so isolated living out in the country, not knowing anyone but my family and a few church people. I was trying to portray that I was perfectly ok, that I was the perfect pastor's wife, not let anyone know of my weakness. I didn't want them to think less of me or hinder my husband's ministry. I was overwhelmed trying to live, which created more anxiety that everyone would find out. I thought everyone would think I was a weak Christian.

I knew God's Word said He would deliver and heal me, but I would read the Word, speak the Word over the situation, but it would not get any better. I felt like I was failing my husband, myself, my son, and God.

I often thought if something was physically wrong with me, like a bad gallbladder or something, it could so easily be fixed with surgery or medication. It could be revealed in an X-ray or by blood work. There would finally be a fix for it. So I went to the doctor and the cardiologist, knowing something was wrong causing this heart to race and all this anxiety. They did find a mitral-valve prolapse, but that was still not the main culprit. I was given meds for the slight heart issue thinking that would fix it all. It helped, but anxiety seemed to still be there.

Feeling more defeated than ever that this was not the issue of this anxiety made me even more anxious. This could not be seen by doctors or by man. It was a spiritual battle and could only be won in the spirit.

I can remember feeling so hopeless, and one day I finally got so MAD at the enemy I said, "You are not destroying my life, my family, or my husband's ministry." I got determined to take my life back!

I wish I could say it was an instantaneous fix, but it was the first step to *rising* up out of my anxiety prison. I finally started to take my life back one day at a time. I started to drive my car by myself a mile and turn around, and then I would go two miles, and then so on.

I can remember going down our long driveway onto the road, and my heart would start to race, and I would feel like I was going to pass out. I even felt trapped at church, thinking I was going to pass out during a service and make a scene. What a fake prison the enemy had me living in. I finally got MAD and yelled at the top of my lungs, "Satan, I rebuke you!"

My husband told me once a powerful example that stayed with me. He said, "Honey, count out loud to ten." I said, "What?" He said, "Count to 10 out loud." So I did, and then he said, "Say your ABCs at the same time you are counting to 10." I said that it was impossible and expressed that I couldn't do both at the same time. He said, "Exactly. When you begin to feel that fear or anxiety come upon speak OUT LOUD the Word of God or pray in tongues, it will silence the fear because your brain can't do both things at the same time." Praise God! That changed my life forever.

As I started doing a simple task, like driving, and I would begin to feel that anxiety, I followed the advice and began to speak the Word aloud. I began to change my circumstances by speaking the Word of the Lord! Proverbs 18:21 NKJV says, "Death and life are in the power of the tongue, and those who love it will eat its fruit." There is life and death in the power of your tongue. Speak life over whatever circumstance you may be in. His Word created the heavens and the earth, and it is still creating and working today! Get BOLD!

After a few months, I was FREE! Glory to God.

The Word talks about familiar spirits. It has tried to appear a few times over the last 30 years, but I immediately remind the enemy that that battle is over and I won through the love of God.

One of my favorite scriptures:
2 Timothy 1:7 Amplified Bible, Classic Edition
"For God did not give us a spirit of timidity (of cowardice, of craven and cringing and fawning fear), but [He has given us a spirit] of power and of love and of calm and well-balanced mind and discipline and self-control."

That's right. I am not timid or afraid. I am full of His power and His love. Glory to God! Whom the Son sets free is free indeed.

I think so many times we think we can confess a scripture around once in a while, and that will do it. Some battles require you to dig deep, lean, and trust God. He loves you so very much. He will never hurt you or withhold any type of healing from you. He is a GOOD, GOOD, God!

I pray this helps someone who is struggling with fear or anxiety.
- Get BOLD.
- Speak the Word out loud over your situation.
* He has already won the Victory, and so have YOU!

I love you, and you are an overcomer!

About - Diane Hoffman

Pastor Diane Hoffman is a Co-Pastor with her husband Gary of Faith Fellowship Church in Wirtz, Virginia. Diane and her husband have been pastoring Faith Fellowship for over 30 years. Raised in the Midwest, she moved to Virginia in 1992 with her husband and Son. Their church grew from a small country church with 30 people to now over 900.

She was not raised going to a local church, and once she encountered the wonderful gift of Salvation and was filled with the Holy Spirit, she experienced a confidence and peace she didn't have before. She went from being very shy and avoiding any type of speaking to now confidently ministering the Word of God.

She has traveled and ministered in Brazil, Costa Rica, Dominican Republic, and Nicaragua on mission trips. Her passion is the prayer ministry, where she leads the women's prayer team at their church. Wherever she goes, her compassionate heart and love for the people are very evident. Her heart is to serve God and to share the love of God with others she comes in contact with.

Along with pastoring, she is also a successful realtor, along with her husband. In just two short years, she has won awards and has been taken outside the church walls and renewed fire for winning souls after seeing how lost and hurting so many people are.

Pastor Diane Hoffman
Faith Fellowship Church
100 Wirtz Rd.
Wirtz, VA 24184
Email: diane@faithfellowship.net
Facebook: www.facebook.com/diane.hoffman.71
Instagram: pastordhoffman

Greater Purpose and Power in Your Pain

By Shonna Slatten

*H*ave you ever gone through a season where you were in an intense battle? A time of great pain and uncertainty? A time when you feel like many things in life are resisting you? A time when the pressures of life seem to keep coming wave after wave. Or perhaps you have experienced pain from deep losses in your life—the loss of a loved one, the loss of a dream, the loss of a beautiful season in your life that was truly a blessed season? The experience is so personal, deep, and painful that it is hard to share or be around others sometimes, so you begin to withdraw and hide because YOU ARE BATTLING! You're in a difficult place, processing multiple situations and changes that suddenly come all at once.

Maybe your family has gone through a trying time, and fear, doubt, and worry have tried to grip you. Maybe you have experienced heartache or a great disappointment in your life, and you're feeling frustrated, angry, and alone. Whatever painful situation you find yourself in, we all want to know: Do I have what it takes within me to make it through this painful, most challenging time? Do I have what it takes to make this major transition in my life? Do I really trust God?

It's when the storms of life come and a major transition forces its way into your life that you find yourself asking these questions and fighting not only for the very existence of purpose in your life but fighting the good fight of faith for your destiny and your inheritance. Whether you're aware of it or not, how you answer this question carries life-changing significance for you and the people around you. The direction of your life will be determined by your actions, depending on how you answer this question. THIS is where your faith is tested, refined, and purified.

It's in these raw, dark seasons, these trying times in our life, that God takes us through a process, and our faith is perfected. In these moments, we may feel crushed, broken, possibly even despaired, hopeless and angry. We can't seem to find our footing or our fit because everything has changed and we feel stripped from what we have known in the daily routine of our lives.

If you say, "This is me. You are describing my life right now," you need to know there is a GREATER PURPOSE and POWER in your PAIN. You are not alone. God is right there with you in the place of brokenness and pain, hopelessness and despair, depression and loneliness. He's in that place of transition or perhaps that fiery trial with you, and He will bring you through to the other side. God is doing a bigger work. He is doing a deeper work in you. He is purifying and refining. Come up higher and look at the bigger picture.

Recently, in my own life, I have gone through some very painful, heartbreaking moments, along with a season of a major transition that has lasted longer than I anticipated. I found myself in a very challenging season going through one of the most trying times in my life. I was walking through some health issues and the loss of family and friends. And at the same time, the Lord was uprooting me from the ministry assignment He had given me for years and bringing great change in my life. I had to find a new normal, and it was rough. The grieving at times was so painful, and the enemy wasn't cutting me any slack. He was buffeting me from all sides. This was a time in my life that called for a great place of surrender once again in my life and a strong shield of faith! It was a fresh surrender to the new thing God wanted to do in my life. It brought me to a greater trust on a different level. God wasn't doing things in my life the same way He used to, and I needed to surrender to the flow of the plan He was trying to lead me in for this next season. I needed to surrender to the process in this season.

It's in times like these that your emotions and fear try to overtake you, and even insecurities try to arise. You can find yourself alone and in a depression going through the motions while crying out to God, "Where are You, God?" I knew He was with me because the Word says in Heb.13:5, He will never leave me nor forsake me, but He seemed to be so silent.

Eventually, I heard the Lord say, "I am here, but the enemy has come to sift you like wheat, but I have prayed for you that your faith fails you not! He has come to buffet you and to test you. But you will come through this time of testing and come out with power and as pure gold for My glory!"

At this time, I really had to press to contend for my destiny like never before! I could not see clearly. It seemed the blueprint had disappeared. As I cried out to the Lord, He ministered to me once again that my faith was being tested in this time of great transition. And I can say it truly was being tested from all sides. Everyone will go through times of testing. That's why our faith is so important because it lets us know the outcome. When we meet that test in faith, we know the outcome is going to be victory.

Victory belongs to us because Jesus already won the victory, but we have to bring our faith to that victory. Faith doesn't mean the absence of tests. It means you know the outcome of the test. And YOU determine the outcome of the test, not the circumstance. There are those challenging times, those fiery trials and pressure, and even sometimes moments of great pain and crushing that your faith is tested, refined, and purified. The Bible says in 1 Peter 1:7, "These trials will show that your faith is genuine. It is being tested as fire tests and purifies gold—though your faith is far more precious than mere gold. So when your faith remains strong through many trials, it will bring you much praise and glory and honor on the day when Jesus Christ is revealed to the whole world."

The truth is that pain is inevitable. Nobody makes it through life without pain. Every person has been crushed at one time or another. It comes to everyone's life, but it never stays. And though the Lord didn't bring the pain in your life that has crushed you, He will use this time in your life to strengthen you and build endurance in you to go the distance—to last. Interestingly, grapes must be crushed to make wine. Grapes crushed in their original state would only last one season. It would rot on the vine. But if you crush the grape and let it ferment, it will last hundreds of years. There is something that happens to us when we are crushed. It builds resilience and tenacity in us that we wouldn't have.

It is the thing that opposes you in the weight room that builds your muscles. It's resistance training. I don't need the weights to cooperate; I need them to resist me. So when life resists you, you GET STRONGER. You get wiser, and you turn into something that can be "kept" that will LAST. You are only strong because of the weight that has been put on you. You would not be the woman you are today if you hadn't gone through some things, suffered, and endured some things.

The enemy would desire moments of pressure to destroy us, but when we turn to God, we allow the pressure to turn us into diamonds. What makes diamonds so strong is also what makes them so intriguingly beautiful. Intense heat and pressure. As with diamonds, so it is with you and me. Life's challenges bring our true worth, value, and strength to the surface. The incredible pressure we face during these fiery trials causes the hidden treasure within us to emerge. A diamond's resilient nature makes it stable, pure, and strong. God uses the intensity of challenging, sometimes painful times and the force of adversity to remove every impurity that would otherwise both weaken our spiritual walk. When you finally emerge from the very darkest, crushing, breaking experiences in your life, you emerge the strongest and the brightest you've ever been. God uses that pressure and turns it into power for His glory.

Peter said in 1 Peter 4:12, " Beloved, do not be amazed *and* bewildered at the fiery ordeal which is taking place to test your quality, as though something strange (unusual and alien to you and your position) were befalling you. (AMP) God is not sending this opposition to test you, but during times of testing, He will remove and build things in you. It's the enemy testing you to see if you really believe what you say you believe. This test has come to test the quality of your faith. That's why we not only need to speak the Word, but we need to be a doer of the Word by taking action. We need to KNOW His promises. It's imperative that we have a solid footing on what we know. If you know something, believe it, and stand on it, it will happen. It won't happen for everybody. It will only happen to those who know it, believe it, stand on it, expect it and act on it. You expect God to move! People go through some things, but you can't let things stop you from the greater cause. We can't let anything stop us from moving forward in the things of God!

During these times of testing in my own life, I kept the answer I knew in God's Word before me, spoke it out with authority, and began to praise God continually with my whole heart. I'm not talking about just going through the motions and praising Him out of your head. I'm talking about praising Him with everything you have within you. As I surrendered to God's process and fought the good fight of faith, He healed, transformed, strengthened, and empowered me for the next assignment. Through exercising my faith, the enemy wasn't able to keep from me what God had promised
me.

The truth is grapes must be crushed to make wine, and diamonds are formed under Pressure. Pearls are made from an irritation, olives are pressed to release the oil, and seeds grow in the darkness. Our faith is tried in the fire of affliction, and growth comes out of dark, hard situations. It's in those times a great transformation takes place. No matter what furnace, trial, or transition you find yourself in, you will be stronger and wiser than ever before because God will cause you to prevail! He makes whole the crushed and broken-hearted. He turns pressure into power. He makes wisdom out of the mistakes we have made and brings an abundant supply of all provisions needed. He refines us and brings us out as pure gold for His glory!

I want to speak to the pain in your life. Sometimes we have a pain, a trauma, or a place that even a counselor is not reaching. But the Holy Spirit lives in you and will get into the deepest chambers of your heart and soul, and He will heal you there. My prayer for you is that you see you have it in you to get through this time. God has not left you, He is with you. That the crushing you feel will bring forth a fresh new wine, and you will come through this dark season changed and transformed like a caterpillar is metamorphosed into a butterfly. That you see, there is a greater purpose and power in your pain, and through that, God will bring you into greater purpose in this next season.

I'm praying for you that your faith fails you NOT in this time of testing. I declare you will come forth like pure gold, and you will see that your faith is genuine. Keep speaking God's promises in His Word. He will bring it to pass and bring you through!

About - Shonna Slatten

Shonna Slatten is an internationally known minister, speaker, and author, who shares a message of faith, unlocking your purpose, and walking in your calling. She encourages individuals to know their position in Christ and to know the Spirit of Truth and His power that is available today. Her influence reaches individuals, organizations, businesses, and nations.

Her international reach has taken her to many nations ministering in churches, women's meetings, Bible schools, and crusades throughout the years. She has been blessed to have the opportunity to travel and serve overseas with Donna Schambach in various churches and crusades. She is an ordained minister, having served in her local church in various positions for over 15 years. She has also served as a spokesperson for several non-profit organizations, emceeing various events, and has ministered on a local cable TV network.

Shonna communicates with clarity, boldness, and passion. Her first book, "Destiny Etched Within, speaks to purpose and destiny. Her passion is to equip and empower individuals beyond the church and into the fullness of their influential purposes in order to further establish God's Kingdom.

Shonna is a graduate of Rhema Bible College and Schambach School of Ministry. She received her Bachelor of Science degree at the University of Oklahoma and has practiced as a dental hygienist for 29 years. Shonna now resides in Norman, Ok.

Contact Shonna at:
http://www.shonnaslatten.org/

Unforgiveness, the Need for Justification, and the Surprise Answer By Eve Ropiecki

It was a critical season in my life and ministry where I was facing, on repeat, feelings of deep disappointment and painful betrayal by people who claimed to be my friends. People who even claimed to be my brothers and sisters in Christ. They had misused, mistreated, lied about, and abandoned me and our friendship, which I highly valued. As I stood yet again in this place of relentless pain, I asked, "God, why haven't you justified me? All I ever did was love these people, and then they abused me and walked away, and now they point their finger back at me!? How can you let this happen!?" It was a question I had asked time and time again.

I didn't always feel hopeless. In fact, God's goodness was abundant in my life. I was surrounded by love and friendship and united with some of the most amazing people. We were getting to do beautiful things together that were fulfilling the dreams in our hearts. It wasn't that I lacked blessings; it was that in spite of all the blessings, I still felt completely unjustified. I felt like it was unfair that God would let people who call themselves Christians mistreat, sow division, and tear His people and His church apart just to walk out the door and head to the next church down the road and spew more lies back my direction when the truth was that all I ever wanted for them was the best.

It wasn't that I thought I was a faultless or perfect person. I knew my weaknesses as well as anyone. I mean, I also knew their weaknesses as well as anyone, but in spite of it all, I would have stood by their side through anything. I would have forgiven anything. I would have fought through anything, and what really got me was how not only did they not fight for our relationship, but they so easily and viciously stabbed me in the back and left me for dead. My friends. Like, my actual friends. It hurt like a bad word. And every once in a while, when the pain would re-emerge, I would find myself again asking God how he could sit by and not justify me.

In my quest for answers and freedom from this pain, I started to take a deeper look at Jesus on the cross. I saw that he never actually was given any kind of justification in the flesh. He even hid from it upon His resurrection. Think about it. He was NEVER justified to the worst of the worst. For all they knew, they killed Him, and He was dead, and that was that. He didn't get up out of the grave and appear to all His haters as a big genie god, laugh in their faces, and kibosh them straight to hell. No, he overcame death, rose victoriously, and stole away to his little crew of the faithful. He never sought justification for all the lies, all the slander, all the accusation, and hatred that was spewed at him. Wow.

As I started to process this whole scenario, it brought me some comfort. If they did it to Jesus, I should be glad to be counted with Him! I tried to hype myself up on this thought, but it only brought partial comfort. It still wasn't exactly erasing the pain. It was an awesome revelation that changed my thinking for the good, but the feeling of wanting to be justified lingered. At least Jesus got to go kick some devils out of heaven and do some cool spiritual ninja stuff!

Still, I longed to be justified. I longed for God to swoop out of heaven and do something that made me feel like loving people who chose to hate and abuse me wasn't all in vain.

Sometimes we really try to candy-coat Christianity with niceties and things that have some truth to them but are ultimately not helpful at all and mostly insincere:

"You just have to love them to death."

"Forgive them, sister, just like Jesus forgave you."

"It's all about love."

"Love, love, love."

Barf.

When you've really been beaten down by people being actually terrible to you for no reason, Christian clichés go right out the window. Yes, you absolutely do have to forgive others the way Jesus forgave you, but forgiveness doesn't always mean you can actually look at those people without searing pain.

They were intentionally vicious, hurt you on purpose, and were not sorry. Beyond forgiveness, you need freedom from that pain, friend.

Sometimes, people may hurt you, but they want to work through the problem together and find peace. That's honestly easy. It's super easy to feel good about getting over a hurdle with someone who wants to make things right even if they've hurt you. It's easy to forgive a heart that wants restoration and healing. But guess what? Not everyone wants that. Just being honest. Some Christians will burn you so badly, then walk out the door and keep talking smack about you all the way down the road to the next church, and the next, and the next. And sometimes, they're not just attending the next church; they're leading it. They're leading the church of Jesus Christ and still spewing hate. Oof. It's a different ball game when the abuse continues, and you're left with your perpetually open wounds trying to forgive and heal. It's not happy-clappy. There are no shortcuts to ease that kind of pain, and I think that when people try to glaze over these ultra-hard realities we face as Christians with catchphrases, they aren't really doing anyone any favors.

No, I knew there had to be more. There had to be an answer to this hurt that I couldn't seem to conquer. I knew that somewhere in the heart of God was the solution, but I couldn't find it. I questioned myself unendingly. I overturned every stone in my mind, trying to see where I could have been wrong enough, bad enough of a friend, terrible enough as a leader to somehow deserve to be treated like dog poo. I couldn't find it. I was totally and absolutely committed to people. I was completely committed to working through every and any offense and hurt and coming out the other side stronger. I was a loyalist to the end. But the thing was, they didn't want anything to do with that. They even hid their faces from me. They wouldn't face me. They didn't try to work anything out. They ran my name through the mud, didn't feel bad about it, and didn't stop.

JUSTIFICATION! Where was my justification?
"I thought if I did the right thing and honored you, you would justify me, God!? But here I am, feeling as unjustified as ever."

And then it came. One day it came. The voice of God spoke straight to my heart, and when He answered, it almost seemed too simple. I kind of felt foolish because I should have figured it out myself. I should have easily been able to come to that conclusion on my own. I thought my intellect should have been able to muster this one up. But I needed to hear it from Him. I needed it to be so real and tangible that I felt it right from His heart to mine. The question rang out in my soul, "Why are you letting me be hurt and disappointed by people?" and His answer came in the still softness of His loving kindness. He said, "Eve, don't you think I was hurt and disappointed, too?"

"Don't you know that they didn't just do the wrong thing to you, but they did the wrong thing to us all? I love them, they're my kids, and I'll always love them and fight for them. I'll never stop leading and guiding them into a better place but what they did in that situation hurt me too. I had plans for them to overcome, but they didn't. I still want them to overcome, and they will, but then and there, they didn't. And it hurt me just like it hurt you because I have plans for this world, and they're a part of those plans, but I need people who are so submitted to me and my will that they won't fail."

"What about you, Eve? Will you let this stop YOU from fulfilling my will? Will you keep going around and around this mountain and be stunted and stifled, or can I trust you to do the right thing and overcome? Can I trust YOU with my plans?"

I felt a paradigm shift, and suddenly my whole outlook and perception of who God was, was different and new. See, I was looking at God as some kind of heavenly sugar daddy who was handing out justification like lollipops. Like He was up there playing chess with the world and, for some reason ignoring my pain and unwilling to meet my need. But at that moment, I caught a glimpse of the God I had known all along but had lost track of. The one who didn't send his son into the world through some royal family who owned all the armies and ruled the kingdoms. He didn't send his son into human authority and power. He didn't do the work of redemption through some kind of micromanagement of the cosmos. No, he was the God who sent his son, the Savior of the world, into obscurity, poverty, scandal, and into one of the most disadvantageous circumstances possible. This wasn't a God who was looking to take easy-street. This was a

God who worked through the unexpected and unconventional. He's always found on the road less traveled because the outcome He's looking for, then and now, isn't just to put on a light show and attract as much attention as possible so all the groupies will start to praise Him.

No, the outcome he's after is a people of faith. And faith, like a diamond, isn't produced out of ease and glamor; it's produced out of pressure and dirt. The down and dirty, the pressure cooker, if you will, is what pops out those sparklers. And faith comes in much the same way. It comes through the crushing. It comes through the trial and the wait. It comes through disappointment with perseverance. It's born out of a heart that's so sold out it's willing to endure inconvenience and discomfort to reach the end goal.

Faith isn't cheap, and God's not after what's cheap. He's after a people willing to stick it out, those who are not in it for their own selfish ambition or their own justification in the flesh but those who are in it for Him and with Him. He's after people who are willing to follow through with His plan even when it doesn't feel good or look glamorous. He's after people who are so past their own agendas and so submitted to Him that it doesn't matter what it costs them. They're in it for more than their own reputation, opinions, and ideas. If it means they're inconvenienced at times and have to pick up their cross and bear it, so be it. They're ready to rejoice in the face of persecution because they are those who are willing to follow at any cost.

I now live my life in a posture of thanksgiving and praise, and I'm free to forgive and love even in the face of persecution because I have the heart of my Father. He's not only my defender but also my ally and friend. We're in this thing together to the end. My mission is to see people set free from the bondage of the opinion of man and liberated to live and do the will of God in peace and in joy no matter what comes their way, to truly live the victorious life that Jesus purchased with his blood. The victorious life isn't our current set of circumstances. It's our identity. It's our birthright.

About - Eve Ropiecki

E ve Ropiecki was born and raised in upstate NY, where she was mentored faithfully under her father's ministry from youth to adulthood. She attended Hillsong College in Sydney, Australia, where she received her certification in ministry. After graduating, she returned to Binghamton, NY, where she was ordained and now serves as worship and women's ministry pastor at United With Christ, Johnson City, NY.

As a worship pastor, Eve has led her team in writing and recording many original songs and the release of their debut album, From The Beginning. As a women's ministry pastor, Eve hosts a vibrant women's conference each year, which brings together women from all over the country to be encouraged and equipped.

She also serves on the oversight team of apostolic network, United With Christ International, through which she has helped to plant multiple churches, raise up local worship teams, and provide ongoing support through the preaching of the word.

Eve is a powerhouse speaker and always delivers an in-season word that brings clarity and freedom. She has traveled the country ministering at churches and conferences and has a passion for using her gift to serve the body of Christ at large.

Eve and her husband, Mark, have been married for 16 years and have three beautiful children, Jackson, Scarlett, and Savannah. Eve also homeschools all three of her children, is actively involved in her local Classical Conversations community and has served as a director and tutor for many years.

You can connect with Eve
Facebook, Instagram @EveRopiecki &
@WordsWithEve,
or via email at EveRopiecki@gmail.com

He Came in Presence
By Sherry Cecil

—⁓◦◦◦⁓◦◦◦⁓—

When I was a child, I was a victim of sexual abuse, sadly enough it is not uncommon, but put that on top of other social disorders from living in the backwoods of Kentucky (in ways that were even foreign to the day I was living), you get a child with a very broken spirit.

I had an outside family member who became abusive and began to mishandle me when I was very small. I was around four years old, and when he would come to me, he would always tell me he loved me, but if I ever told anyone what he was doing, no one would love me anymore. This put my life on a loveless path of fear, shame, pain, and guilt. I felt very robbed of life. As a preschooler, I picked my thumbnails from nerves until I had to have them removed because they got so infected. I also had yeast infections over and again as a child. The doctor seemed to know something was wrong, but I was in a sealed room. I couldn't speak of this to anyone. I was so fearful of never being loved.

My family was not an active church-going family. I would go on occasions with someone. Mom loved Jesus, the Bible, and gospel songs. But she only had a fourth-grade education and was not very churched, so all we knew was there was a God, a Devil, and Jesus Loved me this I know. But there was never enough truth given me to free me.

One day, I went into the bathroom, where no one could see me cry. To cry was a weakness in our home, and as I sat there crying, I looked out the window, and it seemed the sky had opened. There was this person whom I (somehow) knew to be Jesus, and he was smiling at me. I was crying, and he was smiling. He affirmed me and comforted me. He came to me. That was the first encounter I ever had with Jesus, and it stuck with me.

But I was still very broken and socially backward, except when any man wanted to pay attention to me. I had become very promiscuous from the abuse. I could not say "no" to any man who wanted to have his way with me. It was all I knew that love was, and I wanted to be happy and loved more than anything. So I went from one man to the next. I was prey for every lowlife around. I would give all of me only to be dropped by them and mocked by mockers.

I wanted a life like I saw others enjoying, but I couldn't because something in me was so broken, and my life was such a mess. I became entangled with drugs and alcohol to try to fill the emptiness. But I had a void that nothing could fill. And no person could heal. There were layers and layers of my life that needed to be reconstructed and restored. Abuse will leave you torn to shreds, and then people who pass by will make you feel like you are the scum of the earth. When all you want is for someone to stop and say I can help you, someone, to show you what it really means to be loved.

Finally, when I was in my twenties, I went to bed like any other night when I was awakened. I opened my eyes, and the room was full of light, and the most wonderful peace I had ever experienced washed over me. As I looked around, a man stood next to my bed. He was clad in a robe of royal purple. The sleeves of the robe were draped over the hands, and the tunic covered his feet. I do not recall a face. I was in a trance-like state, and I could not move or talk. And then I heard a voice. It came from above saying, "This is Jesus." It was like being properly introduced to someone for the first time.

The man raised his arm and from beneath the flowing sleeve of the robe was a scroll being handed to me. As I reached for the scroll, I was released from the trance-like state, and it was all over. The room was now just as dark as it was at bedtime.

I remember jumping up and running to the living room, where a large family Bible lay on the coffee table. It was a mere decoration and had never been read. It was just the fashion statement of the day. But today, I opened it, and when I did, it fell open to Ezekiel Chapter 3. It was there that these Words were penned, "Son of man eat what you find here, and go and speak to the house of Israel. So I opened my mouth and he fed me the scroll. Son of man feed your stomach, and fill your belly with this scroll that I give you. So I ate and it was like honey in my mouth."

I knew then that this scroll was the written Word, the Word that I grew to love as much as the Spirit Author. Finally, someone had come to help me and to show me what love really was, but it was not a person on the street. It was Jesus. When no one would stop, when no one would help, He came in presence!

After this, I soon found my way into a Church where I was born again, and I began to heal and learn to forgive both others and myself. How did my healing take place? It was one day at a time. I was one service at a time. It was one Bible reading at a time. It was one leading of the Spirit at a time.

I would go to church every time the doors were opened. I would sit and read my bible every day and allow the Word and the Holy Spirit to speak into my life.

I would be prompted to get up around 3 am every morning and just sit with the Word and allow the Holy Spirit to commune with me and heal me. My healing was not natural, any more than my salvation. It was supernatural. People may not always understand this or accept it, but it is my truth. And it is the truth that set me free, healed me, and gave me a wonderful husband of over 34 years now, a husband who has been faithful to me and to whom I have been faithful. We have a strong and healthy marriage, with two children, three grandchildren, and two great-grandchildren.

It is not always a counseling session or a medication that we need. It is truth, love, and a relationship with Jesus.

I am not against medicine, counseling, or any natural means of recovery. But for me, I cried, and He heard me. He came to me in my presence. He came and walked with me and talked with me. He took me from the grueling waters of the aftereffects of sexual abuse and social dysfunction and taught me how to live, and set me on a path of success.

He came with my antidote and my promissory note. Everything that he promised me in His Word He has done. He saved me, filled me, healed me, prospered me, and set me in a home. He gave me joy and set me on a path of life with true love guiding me. There is a balm for your soul (mind, will, and emotions) if you are willing to call out to Him.

About - Sherry Cecil

Sherry Cecil is the Associate Pastor and Prayer Director of Life Fellowship Church in Bowling Green, Kentucky, and recently accepted a Team Leadership position with FCF.

She graduated Domata School of Missions in 1999. In 2005 she was ordained through Faith Christian Fellowship of Broken Arrow, Oklahoma, under Dr. Pat Harrison.

Sherry has ministered both nationally and internationally, traveling to places such as China, Mexico, Mongolia, Sweden, Kazakhstan, and the UAE, where teams were set up to preach the gospel, win the lost, pray for the sick, distribute literature, and reach communities.

Her passion is to teach people the truth in a practical and often poetic way, and her greatest reward is sharing Jesus effectively so that others grow to know the love of God and reciprocate it.

Sherry Cecil
sherrylynncecil@gmail.com
270-776-7818

Rescued
By Rachel Reboul

he day my walk and my life began to change was the day I said "Yes" to Jesus and the day I began to embrace healing. I had done inner healing because I knew there were many things on the inside that were keeping me from experiencing God's love.

Let's rewind to 2015 when I said, "Yes." When I was a little girl, I asked God into my heart. I was saved and baptized. I loved God, and I remember telling my Mom I was going to read the whole Bible. I started on Genesis 1:1 as a nine-year-old and went right to sleep. My parents were believers, and we would go to church Sunday morning, Sunday evening, and Wednesday nights. There was what felt like a bomb that went off in our home. Not so much in the natural, but definitely the spiritual. The day the bomb went off for me was the day I found out my parents were getting a divorce. I remember my Mom not telling me everything, but enough to know that my Dad could possibly have a girlfriend and that now we could only see him with adult supervision. I remember hopping on the phone and telling him I would no longer call him Dad but by his name. I was broken. He saw me two times after the divorce and saw me again when I went looking for him when I was 18. When I saw him when I was 18, he told me he would always try to leave my Mom, but she would end up pregnant. I was rejected and abandoned at nine years old. I was a young girl that had a love for God but developed a hate toward men.

I didn't know much about Satan and his demons, but I believe they did come to steal, kill and destroy my family. At this time, I picked up a spirit of abandonment, rejection, self-pity, and an orphan spirit. My Mom became bitter as the bomb went off. Mom had four children, went back to school, and worked a couple of jobs to help support her family that my Dad walked out on. My Dad told my Mom that he would see her and my siblings in the gutter.

In this new season that we were all learning to live in, Mom was working on weekends, and the church was no longer a priority. I believe with all the roots of anger and bitterness I had; I wasn't able to pursue or seek God.

During this season of working, Mom trusted many she shouldn't have. I remember one day, my Dad tried to check me out of school without permission. It was a pretty dramatic experience. My Mom sent my brother and me to stay at a friend's house. This guy began to kiss me in my ear, and when I went to bed, I woke up, and his hands were in my pants. When I woke up, I was mad, and he told me he was playing a game. I lost it. You see, this wasn't the first time that I had been taken advantage of by a man doing something he wasn't supposed to be doing to me. From the time I could remember, I was being molested by our neighbor, who I called PaPa.

Fast forward to adulthood. I was married and divorced to a man who was 19 years older than me. I was not saved, and I was looking for a Daddy or someone to take care of me. I had no idea how deep-rooted my childhood came into play in my adulthood, which underlined that I had a hate for men. I had no idea my body was a Holy temple, and I slept with men to fill a void and find love. It literally left me feeling even more empty. Battling depression, I could hardly get out of bed, and I had thought of suicide. All of these things from the world just left me feeling even more empty and alone. I remember one time thinking of suicide and grabbing my dusty Bible and reading the red words of what Jesus said.

I would go through multiple relationships, and none really ever worked. I really felt like I was done dating, and I would focus on my career until the day I met my now husband. I remember thinking there was something different about him, and I did not want to not be around him. I kept him in the friend zone for a while, of which he was not a fan. We were both not saved, although I thought I was.

In 2015 we gave our lives to God. He seemed to be seeing rainbows and butterflies, but I had an interesting time, to say the least. I dove in, and I mean all in. I remember seeing something that was cursing God's name. I went to see our prayer pastor, explained everything to him, and he smiled and said I was radical.

I was not one foot in and one foot out but all in. One week I was watching shows that the next week I simply could not. I legit felt like my eyes were burning when I tried to watch it. I really fell in love with the Father, I put the things of this world down, and I wanted to go all in with Him. I had done it my way, and it did not work. I began to read my Bible, and I made it passed Genesis this time. God sent some amazing women of God to help me on my walk. I remember one day I did not answer my phone, and one of my God friends sent me a message saying she was on her way, and I quickly answered the phone. At that moment, I knew she was a God send, and she was exactly what I needed in that season. We are all still friends to this day, and our kiddos are like family. I remember one friend telling me God loved me like a Father. I was thinking, "Oh, no, I sure hope not," mine walked out on my family and me. At this time, I had my first two boys, and I would put them on the floor to play and dive into His word. I would learn how to pray, I would study the commandments, and I would dive into how to pray the tabernacle prayer.

I remember wanting to fly to Florida to see someone who was anointed, and I wanted to see what it was like to fall out in the Spirit. My husband thought I was nuts, but I wanted to see all of what God had. Literally, the next week a pastor from out of town came to our church and called me out of a crowd of about 1,000 people, which I still believe to this day I needed. He said, "God doesn't care about your past. He loves you and does not even remember it." It was easier for me to forgive others, but when it came to myself, it was not easy.

During this time, I joined a Bible study with an amazing woman of God. She had been saved for a while, and I genuinely trusted her with all of me. One day during our Bible study, we got into a prayer circle of about four people, and she asked me if I had any special prayer requests, and I did. I told her that when I would get close to the Father, I would feel this perversion. She instantly told me I needed to go through a program that she was leading. As I trusted her, I knew it was something I needed to do.

I did forgive PaPa after I got saved, and I prayed he had repented. Before I was saved, I could not say the same. After about a month of being nervous doing the program, I finally went through it as she stayed with me through text and email. One specific email said, "Don't let satan stop you." I even remember, in this season, asking God to send women who had walked through similar situations that I could help. But honestly, when it was God and me alone, I would ask Him why He picked me to be born to this and in the hands of pure evil. The love for the Father was there, but I could not figure out how to trust Him with what I had walked through.

At the beginning of my session, the lady asked me to go back to Papa's house. I remember feeling anxious, and my body was getting warm and red. However, it had been years since I stepped foot in that house. I hated it. There were parts of this house that I blocked out. In my mind, I go back to the living room, and I see a red balloon. I would see something, and I would instantly know what He was trying to tell me. I would hear, "What does a balloon represent? What is it used for?" And I would know it was used for birthdays or celebrations. I was asked to come out of the house, and the lady asked me what I saw, and I saw Jesus and I running and the Father watching us. The feeling I felt was the happiest joy I had ever felt. He was a shield when I looked up, and no darkness could come near Jesus, and I. God was watching us with so much love and joy. I was asked to go back into the house, and Jesus and I walked past that area that I had blocked out, and I saw myself as a 4-year-old little girl being raped. Jesus had His arm around me, and then He laughed at the demon that tried to destroy me. You see, the same demon that tried to destroy me would turn the situation around on God and lie to me and say, "Where was He? And why didn't He stop it?" After seeing this, I saw a strong arm shoving everything into this round tunnel-looking hole. He was angry and said, "He who touches my daughter - vengeance is mine." At that moment, my heart knew He was angry and that this was not the plan He had for me and that He loved me like a good Father, a heavenly Father, not like a human father that is not perfect.

At this moment, I see rapid water that splits, and the house where this traumatic situation happened is crushed. There was a fruit tree next to PaPa's house. I would have dreams about this tree or nightmares of remembrance. Well, the next thing I see is the tree getting crushed, and to this day, I have not dreamed about that tree. Glory to God. He then showed me a new tree with bright red fruit, and He said, "I'm making all things new." I believed Him, and I trusted Him. I forgave PaPa at that moment for raping me. After this, I had lunch with my husband, and my walk with Jesus began to change as I trusted God that He was a good Father. From this moment, He began to heal me and deliver me, and I began to feel free. I broke ungodly soul ties, I learned to trust, and I forgave an area that I blocked out.

I am now on a beautiful journey that I can trust. I love the Lord, still sold out for Him, reading His word, and hanging unto every promise He has for my children and me. He is a good Father that is loving us, healing us, restoring us, taking us from glory to glory, and working all things out for our good. He loves us with everlasting love, He saves our tears, knows the hairs on our heads, and He is making every crooked path straight and rough place smooth. He is jealous for us. He created us for His pleasure. We are fearfully and wonderfully made, and we are so loved. He never leaves us, nor does He forsake us.

"And if [we are His] children, [then we are His] heirs also: heirs of God and fellow heirs with Christ [sharing His spiritual blessing and inheritance] if indeed we share in His suffering so that we may also share in His glory. Romans 8:17 AMP. "And He who sits on the throne said, Behold, I am making all things new. Also, He said, write, for these words are faithful and true [they are accurate, incorruptible, and trustworthy]." Revelation 21:5 AMP. I pray today that you are encouraged that no matter what you have walked through that He is making all things new, and He loves you so much.

About - Rachel Reboul

Rachel Reboul is the wife of Don and has been married for 11 years. She has four kids and one on the way. Rachel is a passionate entrepreneur in the sales field. With God, she made the top of her company, top in recruiting, top in sales, and top 1% of the company multiple years in a row with over 35,000 co-workers. Rachel led a team of over 500 women and men and has also coached people on how to duplicate what she was doing. Rachel's passion is to evangelize. She also dreams of opening a home for women who have been human trafficked and is the founder of the nonprofit called Let My People Go. Her heart is for the lost. She's cried out many nights to the Father for people to be saved. Rachel wants to lay hands on the sick, and they will be healed, cast demons out, and go to the nations sharing the heart of the Father and that if He did it for me, He could do it for you. "And we know that all things work together for good to those who love God, to those who are the called according to His purpose." Romans 8:28 NKJV

Contact Rachel:
https://m.facebook.com/rachelreboul
https://www.instagram.com/rachelreboul3/
Rachelreboul@yahoo.com

Expecting in the Unexpected
By Jennifer Bosco

Because he has set his love upon Me, therefore I will deliver him; I will set him on high, because he has known My name. He shall call upon Me, and I will answer him; I will be with him in trouble; I will deliver him and honor him. With long life I will satisfy him, and show him My salvation.
Psalm 91:16

The hot sun only intensified as it radiated through the passenger-side window of our minivan. Its reputation of supplying all energy to all living things was not welcome at this moment as it seemed to suck all mine away. My husband and four kids went into Wendy's for an all-too-predictable fast food lunch while the day would be remembered as anything but. I chose to stay behind since my head now pounded painfully from all the crying. I knew I must have shed every tear I possibly could have. I had no expectation when I woke that September morning that my last day at church, on this, my birthday weekend, would end with such tragic heartbreak. I had never felt so angry, sad, mistreated, and even robbed as I did at that moment, curled on my side in the reclined front seat alone with my throbbing thoughts.

We had just experienced our last gathering with the precious people we had served the previous fifteen years in ministry as their youth pastors, children's ministers, worship leaders, and executive pastors. As a long-term ministry couple, we got to cover a lot of bases in those years within a changing, adapting faith organization. The second service was delayed since the single line of strung-out goodbyes from the first service was still in process. Months previous to this day, congregants had asked what was happening as they saw that we had been abruptly removed from our very visible and vital duties to be relegated from serving on the stage to sitting in the second row. One respected elder, WWII veteran, and friend to our family must have discerned the situation since he stopped me one Sunday morning to say that politics can be nasty, "even here."

It wasn't our decision that this would be our last day. It was our colleague's. We had served as pastors together on the same staff for nearly fifteen years. He was our elder by twenty-some years. He had been our ministry school instructor twelve years before. He had gone to Bible training school, whereas we had been ordained and trained on the job. Maybe it was all these things that made him feel that he would decide our future role. There wasn't "a place for us," we were told, but the explanation rang hollow, and the feeling was cold. Maybe we simply were not liked. Maybe we were in the way. Whatever the reason, in a crisis moment in the history of that church, he would stay, and we were being asked to go.

It didn't seem to matter the destiny-affirming words the founding pastor had spoken to us before he retired. It didn't matter that his successor had trained us, encouraged us, and entrusted us with the greatest responsibilities of the entire organization next to his own. It didn't matter the years of knitted and divine heart relationships that were joyfully formed. It didn't matter that to that last day, and beyond, we maintained a future vision for this cherished place and for its people. It didn't matter that even in this greatest pain, we complied with the proposed three-month transition process, not explaining ourselves to the congregation. It didn't matter that on this final morning, blame was publicly placed upon us, and we were given no opportunity to speak. Sitting in that stiff, unyielding, church-row seat, my neck and shoulders tightened instinctively, my stomach writhed with injustice, and blood heat rushed to my ears and brain. I felt absolutely unsettled as I listened to conjured explanations that betrayed our agreement behind closed doors. We walked through those long months virtually unknown.

I was sure I would never gain an appetite to ever eat again. In my depleted, emotional heap, thoughts tore at me like a tempest. Dark, overtaking waves of failure, self-criticism, insecurity, and despair battered my soul and beat upon my mind. Questions blasted, trying to stake claim to my peace. Was this whole moment deserved? What had I done to incur such rejection and abandonment? At forty-two years old, was I to start all over again and somehow find another more palatable me with a better personality and an obviously less-offensive line of work? I had been told I was too much. Too loud. Too intense. Too talkative. Too ambitious. Too intimidating. And in this particular moment, I had begun to believe it all since the circumstances seemed to confirm the accusing words.

For the three and a half years following, every effort made to continue in our work had, for me, an attached, subtle doubt because of the lingering power of those previous words. It was nothing that anyone else might detect since we pioneered a new church and ministry within five months of our transition. At God's direction and by His grace, people were being impacted, and the community was growing. Without the necessity of a second job or a side hustle, our work was blessed. We were thankful to be able to continue in the core work of what we believed was our calling and purpose.

In those years, I knew I needed to establish independence from negative, external words and dependence on God's life-giving, internal words. I needed to batten and brace my very deepest self with words that were truth and grace. Words that were for all, that didn't single me out as one to be pitied, and simultaneously, words that were just for me, that hit my heart with reality as though they were *only* for me. Steadying life words that would become anchored beliefs rather than occasional passing thoughts. Words whose significance was universal yet intimate, eternal yet immediate. Words that held my future and would, in fact, build a stronger me for this new time, a new position, and a new influence.

And in just those same years, like a life preserver thrown in the most necessarily fearful and dangerous time and situation, new friends and ministry associates came to our lives through seemingly-unusual social media interactions, rare reunions in unexpected places, and newly shared ministry spaces. If I had felt unknown among 1,000 proximate people, I was finally feeling known by the few that were being sent. To unexpectedly meet my high school choir director halfway between our 800-mile-distanced homes on a random weekday, thirty years from the last time I'd seen her, only to then have a posted picture from that encounter facilitate a connection with a significant minister, was *so* unimaginable. It would have been almost *unbelievable* if it hadn't actually occurred! That connection that day was pivotal to how I needed to progress from that place at just the perfect time. It was impossible to deny that divine directive was on display, and the deepest longings of connection and common Christ community were now being met in the most beautifully surprising ways. For all the hurt I had felt on that last day of the former season, I now was gaining hope of healing as we forged *this* season.

If God was ever obviously concerned about me and graciously good to care for my needs, it was in this transitional time. There's no way I'd ever be convinced that all that aligned in those days were threads of happenstance and chanced coincidence. It was, rather, the grace and goodness of God on full display for my sense of security and for my success as I expected His help and supply. It was never more evident that favor was being disbursed in my direction just because God is good that way and in every way. In all my messy emotions, with all my questions, and doing what I could to dodge the doubts, He was caring for me and leading my way.

There is such a cherished, child-like quality to being so sure of God and so submitted to His kind and loving nature that one should become careless in the care of the Father. Seasons of life will certainly come and are signaled by many starts and stops, booms and bungles, but there is One Who oversees them all, having established parameters as to the lengths, the processes, the provisions, the colors, the enjoyments, the changes. In the worst of situations, even the grave could not lengthen its hold beyond three days! There, then, becomes in God an excited anticipation, even in the unknown, because He has made Himself known and makes me know I am known. Nothing goes unnoticed, and nothing is without significance to what He is working on in this life story.

Yes, all of it matters. All the submitted service and yielded heart-attitude that preceded that transition time were not forgotten or overlooked. While others may not notice or willingly acknowledge the years of sacrifice and growth that were sown, and in fact, some may even resent it or try to claim it as their own; I learned then that with people is not where my approval and commendation lie. My disappointment revealed my need to primarily transfer my trust from the people of God, however a gift they are designed to be, to the unfailing God of the people. My reliance and assurance were relocated. There can be a tremendous satisfaction knowing a season has ended, and assignments have been fulfilled, but it is solely borne by the individual with whom the responsibility was entrusted, and no one can confer that achievement on another except the One Who issued the assignment from the start.

I now regularly remind myself that, like Jesus, I know my identity, my times, and my purposes. I'm always anticipating growing into greater understanding, and greater expression, with greater opportunity. One place, one time, or one season cannot support all that this life in Christ holds. The unfolding compounds. The knowing becomes exponential. The working out of all these things requires movement and change. How I knew God to work in past seasons only sets the expectation for the wonderfully unexpected things He'll do in the next. Even when the unpredictable happens, count on the graces of His presence, provision, and direction to be all the more revealed. I cried, and He more than delivered!

Be sure I *am* eating (I never stopped, in fact), the sun and I are getting along nicely (it's always welcome to keep shining its rays my way), Wendy's trips are thankfully fewer and far between, and the minivan has been upgraded to a new-to-me SUV. And we, the beautiful Body of Christ, the blessed Church, are expansive, far-spreading beyond one location and time, active in every season to facilitate new adventures and new opportunities to see and tell of the goodness of God. Right in the midst of any and every challenge, and especially in the unforeseen, we find Him altogether trustworthy.

Seasons are undisputedly poetic,
stirring emotions,
prompting reflection,
expectation disarranged.
Had I known they existed beyond botany and biology,
touching more than tides and times,
I would have known to trust the shiftings worked
upon my soul when the sun seemed yet to shine.
Steady yourself when all turns upside down.
Set yourself to change.
Seek to know, and you'll find you're known,
as you call upon His Name.

About - Jennifer Bosco

Having been a pastor, teacher, and home educator for over 25 years, coupled with her experience as a worship leader, vocal arranger, and recording artist, Jennifer Bosco helped to co-found, with her husband, the ministry of Highway Church in New England in 2014. She and her husband, Joseph, then debuted their first album, Seen and Unseen, in 2016, and is featured on all major digital platforms and accessed in over 100 nations. Now based in Tulsa, Oklahoma, they travel with their five adult children and family throughout the U.S., performing their original music in various venues and churches, as well as facilitating praise and worship for conferences and ministry gatherings in a unique and distinct, upbeat style. Their ministry has most recently evolved online to include Highway Home Network, a network of homes and businesses from Boston to L.A. that host weekly public gatherings around the teaching emphasis of Who Jesus Is, What He's Done For Us, and Who We Are in Him. Jennifer also is an Interior Design student who enjoys the creative collision of history, architecture, and period furniture and will enthusiastically engage in a good guessing game of single-origin coffee notes.

Fear Still Had a Home
By Nina Rivera

The Bible teaches us that our Father in heaven is omniscient. Hebrews 4:13 states, "There is not one person who can hide their thoughts from God, for there is nothing that we do remains a secret, and nothing created is concealed, but everything is exposed and defenseless before His eyes, to whom we must render an account" (TPT). He knew you and me from before the beginning of time. He knew what the victories were going to be as well as what the failures would be. And even with Him being aware of the failures, He has not only created us anyway but has sent His redeeming love to capture our hearts. The Bible also teaches us about the enemy of our souls, Satan. He prowls around roaring at us, seeking us out, and attempting to devour us (I Peter 5:8). As much as we would like to discount his ability, one thing for sure is that he is calculated and a good student of our character. He knows what makes us walk out of our Godly identity and what will stumble that same stride.

So here my story begins. Have you ever met a shy child? Well, I was one of those. When in public, I held a quiet demeanor and rarely spoke. It is one thing to be introverted, as this is a character trait by which people gain energy for output by being by themselves. This is who I am. But shyness, I believe, is rooted in fear. As I grew up, this shy girl displayed more and more evidence of this attribute, revealing a root of fear. Through events that took place in my childhood, such as bullying in school, parental addictions, and divorce, the root grew. I was fearful of disappointing my mother, so I became an overachiever at school. I was fearful of the kids at school, so I would dummy-down the way I looked not to attract attention, and I would rarely speak to anyone. Addiction at home caused fear so as not to be the one to set off my father. I was fearful of my mother's former second husband to avoid arguments and discord at home. As a result, I became an adult, and fear took up residence in my heart.

When considering years past, I can think of many times when fear would display evidence that it was still actively working in my life. One of these times occurred in 2009. My wonderful husband and I were married for about nine years, and we were the parents of a wonderful two-year-old little girl. My husband had gotten into a bad car accident involving five or so vehicles and was found to be at fault. Amid the panic and swirling worst-case scenarios, we decided to sell our little home and move in with a family member. We wrestled with angst, anger, disappointment, and delirium regularly. How could our Father in heaven permit such a traumatic experience? The days were long, and the nights even longer during this season.

Within the months ahead, I found myself pregnant with our second child.

I should have been rejoicing, rejuvenating, and celebrating new life in the midst of this difficult season, but instead, I became extremely distraught and unsettled. You see, the spirit of fear had not forgotten my vulnerability. Although I had been walking with Jesus during this time and was very in love with Him, I had not let go of the tendency to fall back on the familiar. I allowed the natural tendency of my flesh and emotions to lead the way. I remember my state of mind was so corrupted by fear that mothering, which was so natural, became burdensome. I would fill my days with complaints about how expensive it was, how emotionally drained I would feel, and how incapable my husband and I were in that season. I came up with every excuse in the book of why having this new baby was a mistake.

One evening while driving alone, I was waiting to make a left-hand turn into the neighborhood where we lived. Without realizing it was coming, a midsize pickup truck ran into our car's back and totaled it. I do not remember a ton from that day, except the overwhelming knowing that I had a baby in my womb that may have been impacted. There came over me a deep sense of angst as I also experienced a fall down a flight of stairs a couple of weeks prior. Between these two events and the current state of fear engulfing me, it was the perfect platform for a disaster. Fear had such a grip on me that during these two events and instead of praying, I became like a little girl who curled herself up in a ball, waiting for the inevitable to occur. Fear took my voice, and little did I realize it had taken it for many years.

I began bleeding shortly after the accident. My husband and I made our way to the hospital, where the doctor had advised that there was no heartbeat. I was provided an option right away to have a dilation and evacuation procedure, as I was already entering my second trimester. I denied the procedure and advised that I would contact my doctor instead. The ride back was excruciating yet eerily quiet. My husband took me to a diner, hoping he could talk with me. But nothing could be said. I was numb, and so was he. I did not cry. I did not scream, although later, I would experience such emotions. But over the next several weeks, I was numb.

Another day or so after the hospital visit, my body went into labor. The entire scene was not the most ideal as we were living in a basement. While the labor pains came and went, there was still not a tear. I had received this event as my portion like it was my punishment. I was convinced that this was my fault for my terrible attitude toward everything. Thankfully, what got me through those hours was my two-year-old daughter. You see, as mommy was moaning and groaning in labor, she constantly played at my feet, summoning me to play with her. So every time my body would break until the next wave of pain, I would sit on the floor and engage in play. She was the break in the clouds during the storm.

After a few hours of this, I gave birth to my baby. My husband received the baby as he or she came out of my womb. I was standing while my mother was beside me, holding me. At the request of the doctor, we placed our precious child in a brown paper bag just several inches long. Upon arrival at the doctor's office, they took my baby, drew some blood from my arm, and promptly sent me home. I was by myself. I remember tears of pain, guilt, and shame pouring down my face during the drive. It felt as if I aborted my baby instead of miscarrying. I could not shake the feeling of this being my fault. The next six months would be filled with quiet numbness, mental haziness, and emotional absence.

When preparing for this chapter, I reached out to my friend of many years. I asked her how my composure was during this time of life, as we were also co-workers. She stated she remembered me being very quiet and seemingly disoriented. She said I would often go into a daze when she would talk with me. "It was totally unlike you. In essence, you were numb," she explained. In hindsight, my emotions were like walking a tightrope. There was great condemnation over me. Guilt and shame were trying to take me over. In my mind, this was my portion. I picked the cards myself, and now I had to play the game.

Yet, on the other hand, there was a great truth that spoke a better word over me. That truth was the goodness of God. You see, up to this point, I could not deny His goodness over my life. And in this season, it became an anthem or a song that started in a soft, low tone, but as the days progressed, the song became louder. I made a decision early in the process to not drown in sorrow but continue forward even in pain. Church, fellowship, prayer, and even work, and family events, I never failed to attend. I pressed through it. The book of Psalms 27:13 (NKJV) states, "I would have lost heart unless I had believed that I would see the goodness of the Lord in the land of the living. Wait on the Lord; Be of good courage; And He shall strengthen your heart; Wait, I say, on the Lord!"

I was processed in a dark, private place. It was my hiding place. Yet thankfully, as the film needs to be developed in a dark room, God and His mighty hand were developing me there. I am thankful for the foundation that the Father built in me previous to this. I knew who I was in Jesus, a daughter. I was fully convinced that He loved me and that He was for me. Although I was enduring this hard season, nothing could rip from my knowing that I belonged to my Father. He was with me in the tears, in the questioning, and in the numbness. When I thought I could not see Him, He was sitting right next to me. He was my counselor, my balm of healing.

It took some time to gain a new perspective. I often do not remember the fall or the accident, but my words during that time of life ring vividly. Proverbs 12:18 (NIV) teaches us that "Reckless words pierce like a sword, but the tongue of the wise brings healing." I honestly do not think that my poor attitude created the loss, but what it created was a perfect storm. I understand that my words, my attitude, and my actions during the pregnancy were filled with bitterness engulfed in fear. I can freely admit that now. Yet the storm brought something to me that may not have been able to be communicated any other way. It was that fear that still had a home in me. In the dark room, Jesus, with all gentleness and kindness, showed me the ugliness I displayed because of fear. And simultaneously, He brought me to a place where I could freely repent of my sin and be free from guilt and shame.

Today, I stand with my head held high as a daughter of the King of Kings and Lord of Lords. I have been forgiven and washed afresh. I hope my story brings you encouragement and even clarity. May it assist you in considering how circumstances of the past may have shaped your present perceptions and ways you react to situations. This story is meant to reveal that even as daughters of God, we can make mistakes and fall back into the familiar. And when we do, our Father is right there with us, waiting for us. He is ready to pick up the pieces of our brokenness, of our mess. He is gentle and kind and forever forgiving to them that come with a contrite heart in meekness. In the book of Psalms 34:18, we read, "The Lord is near to the brokenhearted and saves the crushed in spirit."

About - Nina Rivera

Nina Rivera was born and raised in Southern NJ. She graduated from Woodrow Wilson HS and earned a dual bachelor's degree in sociology and criminal justice from Rutgers University - Camden. Nina has worked in the nonprofit sector with students and in the private sector for major corporate companies. She now works as a supervisor in the public sector for the State of NJ. Nina sits on numerous committees where policy and procedure are written for state and federal programming and operations.

In her teens, Nina regularly assisted at a pop-up soup kitchen. In her 20s, she served at a local juvenile detention center giving life skills classes. Over the years, Nina has experienced being a kid's church teacher to running the department. She was a Bible institute student, graduated then taught for the Moody Bible Institute branch in Southern NJ. She has assisted in youth, administrative, and women's boards. For the last six years, she has served as an associate pastor at Higher Places Ministries in Vineland, NJ. Before that, she ministered as head pastor for three years alongside her husband, Samuel Rivera, in Blackwood, NJ. Nina loves the prophetic. She has been married to her husband, Samuel Rivera, for 22 years, and they have two daughters, Nitalia and Gisela. They are still proud residents of Southern NJ.

From Tears to Triumph
By Missy Pittman

hen I was invited to share a chapter in this anthology, it immediately bore witness to my Spirit, and I knew the timing was right. I have had it on my heart to share my story and ultimately desire to minister to those in need, with needs ranging from feeling their life has no purpose and being on the brink of giving up to those that just need strength to get through the day. I believe the words in this chapter will be God-inspired and that He will have His way by ministering to you as you share along with me in my journey of struggles, pain, and grief that have been turned into joy, peace, and a full and thankful heart by the mercy and grace of our loving Father God.

I was raised in church from a very young age. We were there every time the doors were open. I have vivid memories of Wednesday nights getting there early for dinner in the church basement (let's just say I can still taste the best green beans I have ever had!) The church we attended had a strong mission heart, and some of my fondest memories in that church were when missionaries came in and shared what God was doing on the mission field. It put a desire in my heart to go and experience what they shared, and I was blessed with the opportunity to do so in 2019 in the slums of Tondo in Manila, Philippines. This was a huge turning point in my life. I was 50 years old at the time and had never felt so alive and reminded of how much God loved me and that He had not forgotten me. I was in the center of His plan and right where He wanted me to be in order to minister to those in need. You are never too old to do what God places on your heart. That desire dropped in my heart when I was 9 and 10 years old, and it didn't come to pass until I was 50. Never give up on what God has placed in your heart, even if it appears it can't or won't happen. I am now planning another trip and believe it will be one of many more to come!

We all have a past that involves situations that mold us and shape our very future, and it is what we learn and implement from those circumstances that cause us to walk in the path God has ordained for us. When I was ten years old, my father, who was 35 at the time, suffered a heart attack and died suddenly in the middle of the night. At ten years old, I couldn't fully understand what was happening, and little did I know how extremely hard things would become after that horrible evening. My mom was left to raise my sister (who was three at that time) and me. I remember sitting on our front porch and saying, "Now I'm all alone" I felt so alone and confused about why this had happened. My mom started taking me to counseling because I completely closed myself off from the world, the pain was real, and my heart was broken. I later found out the counselor told my mom that I had locked my heart and thrown away the key. The next few years of life were hard, but during that time in my life, I learned about how much God loved me and how His protective hand was upon me. He showed Himself real to me in many small, subtle ways that became the foundation of my walk with Him.

I was 15 years old and had lost my retainer, my mom was unable to buy me another one, and I knew I needed to be wearing it. I had been given vivid pictures of what my teeth would look like if I didn't wear it, which was enough to ensure I found it! I searched our entire home over, tearing my room apart to no avail. I jumped in the shower and prayed, " God, please help me find this retainer; show me where to look," and I kid you not, it was as clear as day that He said to look in my underwear drawer. I had already dumped that drawer out, but I dried off and opened the drawer and in the bottom, INSIDE a pair of underwear, was my retainer! Something so simple to many but, to me, so powerful because I KNEW He answered my prayers.

After the death of my dad, the following years were tough, my mom did the best she could, but there were so many times I don't know how we would have made it without the help from those in our church for over a year someone mailed my mom $100 each month, at that time $100 was huge! Each month, bags of groceries were delivered, and through the faithfulness of friends and family, He again showed Himself real to me. God is SO faithful. He cares for our every need. There have been many times throughout the years I felt alone and forgotten, but He always came through to remind me He has me in the palm of His hand and that the plans He had for me were not forgotten.

My favorite scripture that has carried me throughout the years is Proverbs 3: 5-6. "Trust in the LORD with all thine heart and lean not unto thine own understanding. In all thy ways acknowledge him and he shall direct thy paths." And that is exactly what He has done! Again, I have shed many tears. I married young and into a family serving in the ministry. My heart was so full, and I was excited about the future. I, like many, dreamed of marrying and becoming a mother. The Lord gave me the desire of my heart, and I have had the privilege of raising three boys. Being a mother to young children was challenging as I did a good part of it alone. My husband traveled and was gone a lot, so I was responsible for a large portion. The enemy is continually looking for those he can destroy, and unfortunately, our marriage did not make it, and after 13 years of marriage, we divorced. What a heartbreaking time for me, but mainly for having to watch the pain and turmoil it caused my children. It was at that time I fell into a depression, I felt again alone, wondering why God wasn't answering my prayers, and I felt so far from Him. I was blessed with many wonderful friends who came through and were there listening and caring for us but, most importantly, praying with me to heal and find direction in my life. Those first two years were hard; my belief and trust in God never wavered, but I felt so far away from Him and what I believed my life was to entail. I studied and got my real estate license and felt it was the path I was to take, I had to support my children and provide, and the door opened and not only opened, but the blessings of God poured out! Ministry is no longer my occupation, but it will always continue to be my calling. God never forsakes us. His plans are far greater than what we can imagine. I chose not to allow bitterness to come into my heart. I truly believe that is why I have been so blessed. I endeavored to keep my heart right and to serve Him.

After being single for a period of time, I met a wonderful caring man that not only loved me but loved my boys as well, we have been married for 16 ½ years, and I'm so very thankful for a loving husband and a man who accepted my children as his own. But the scars of divorce are hardest on the children who have had to live through it. My boys struggled, my heart would break as I saw their pain, and I wanted more than anything to take that pain away. One of my sons had the hardest time accepting and adjusting to his parents separating and, after a time, became addicted to drugs and went down a dark path. It became so bad at times my husband and I were afraid in our own home. We feared for what he might do. One night at 10 pm, I was ironing, and I had a strong unction to go check his room. I searched everything, not really knowing what I was looking for, I searched his room, closet, and the attic of the closet, and as I walked back out of the attic, I peeled back the insulation and found a gun. I know God alerted me to find this preventing something that could have been tragic. But unfortunately, the addiction continued, and his path became darker, ultimately leading him to commit a crime causing him to serve time in prison at the age of 20. The tears seemed to never stop.

I can remember being on the floor in my room one night crying to God, and at that time, I had such a peace come over me, true peace in the midst of the storm. The verse in Ephesians 5:11, 14-17 came to me, and it seemed like such an odd scripture for the situation, but I read it in the Message Bible: "Don't waste your time on useless work, mere busywork, the barren pursuits of darkness...wake up from your sleep..Christ will show you the light! So watch your step. Use your head. Make the most of every chance you get. These are desperate times! Don't live carelessly, unthinkingly. Make sure you understand what the Master wants."

That so spoke to me that the devil wants us to lose focus, to live carelessly, and have the circumstances of life, no matter how devastating they are, distract us from what we are called to do. I encourage you TODAY to remember the desires He has placed in your heart, the plans He has for you to carry out, and GO DO THEM! Regardless of what you are dealing with, wake up from your sleep, wipe your tears and watch God carry you to a life of triumph as He has so graciously done for me.

About - Missy Pittman

For over 18 years, Missy Pittman has been a top-producing multi-million dollar producing real estate agent in the Tulsa metro area. Her passion is helping families with one of their largest financial transactions, and at the same time has been able to minister to those going through trying times or just needing someone to listen, show compassion or pray with them. Missy developed a strong sense of devotion to helping others, and the theme of her business model is "Professional Service; Personal Care," which she has endeavored to incorporate into her everyday life helping others.

Missy holds a degree in Business Management and a minor in Marketing from Oklahoma State University and graduated from Rhema Bible College in

1993. After serving in the ministry for 15+ years, she went through a painful divorce and several years later dealt with a child struggling with addiction which ultimately led to him committing a crime and serving time in prison. Those life challenges changed her and framed her future, pushing her to become all that God had called her to be. She attributes her success in overcoming heartache to not allowing bitterness to enter her heart and keeping God the anchor in all she encounters.

Today she resides in Broken Arrow, Oklahoma, with her husband, Rob. Her greatest accomplishment and joy is being a mom to her three sons, Cameron, Blake, and Skylar, and her grandchildren, Hayes and Haven.

Turning Shame Into Glory: Melissa's Testimony
By Melissa Magyar

I grew up in the small, rural town of Cushing, Wisconsin, with my mom, dad, and younger brother. My parents both grew up on farms, met and married young, and together shared big dreams. After years of hard work, they were coming true; My mom became a successful computer programmer who made purchasing their 3-story lake home with an indoor pool a reality. One of my favorite memories as a child is swimming in the unfinished pool that was temporarily filled with lake water while the house was being built. The water was murky and occupied by frogs, but I didn't care! I spent just about every day after that swimming in that pool; my hair turned green from the chlorine, and I practically grew a fishtail!

My dad partnered with his parents, working the family farm while also taking steps to achieve his dream of becoming a pilot for a commercial airline. He loved to fly! He owned his own small Cessna 172 plane and occasionally took me flying after church. The field he used as a runway was right next door. I can still remember the way the inside of his plane smelled and the pure exhilaration I felt during takeoff when it lifted off the ground. There are no words to describe just how beautiful God's creation looked from the sky! My dad eventually gained enough experience and hours of flight time to earn his commercial license. He needed periodic physicals for medical clearance to fly. During one of his physicals, a chest x-ray detected a small spot on his lung. After several months and further testing, he was diagnosed with Non-Hodgkin's Lymphoma.

My dad received invasive chemotherapy and a very painful bone marrow transplant. He went into remission and was once again determined to get back in the air. He applied for a job with a commercial airline out of Chicago. The day he received the call offering him the job was the exact same day he learned his cancer had come back and was spreading like wildfire. That was the first time he broke down and cried.

After receiving the devastating news, I remember my dad taking me to our church. We walked hand in hand up to the altar, where he knelt and prayed silently. I often wonder what the conversation between him and God that day was like. Did he curse God? Did he beg for his life and miraculous healing? Or did he trust in the Lord and declare, "Thy Will be done." Knowing the kind of man he was, I like to believe it was the latter.

His immune system continued to weaken, and he eventually developed pneumonia. He knew he was dying and that it was time to say goodbye. Some of his last words to my mom and his parents were, "Take good care of my Missy," which is what he called me. He died a few days before my 8th birthday and on his parent's wedding anniversary. The days and months that followed were some of the hardest my family and I have had to endure. The loneliness and debt from all my dad's medical bills weighed heavily on my mom. She didn't want to lose the dream house and the life they had built together. She picked up more projects and hours at work, leaving before the sun rose and coming home after it set. We never lost our home, but rather valuable time with mom.

My grandparents lived just down the road and were also heartbroken over the loss of their son; however, their faith never wavered. They kept their promise to help take good care of us. My brother and I spent many days at their home while mom was working. They were always pouring out their love on us, especially Grandma, who was always sharing God's Word with us. Some of my favorite pastimes were climbing trees, exploring the barn and backwoods, riding a four-wheeler through the corn fields, shooting BB guns at coffee cans, and picking up pinecones in the backyard. Grandpa would pay my brother and me a penny per pinecone to pick them up before mowing the grass. We also spent countless hours with Grandma and Grandpa playing cards, bird watching, gardening, sunbathing on their deck, and helping make apple pies for church.

Our mom eventually met a new man and became engaged after only dating for a short time. He was friendly and engaging when my mom was around but cold and distant when she wasn't. I told my mom this; however, she quickly brushed it off. She thought she was in love and was so desperate to have a father figure back in our home. The marriage was built on a foundation of lies and only lasted four years. My mom discovered he was verbally abusive and had accumulated a mountain of debt. Something good did come out of the marriage, though, the three children from his previous marriage, who were all very close in age to my brother and me. A bond quickly formed, and before long, you couldn't tell us apart from biological siblings. After my mom filed for divorce, they moved out and far away. Once again, we were all left grieving another loss. I was angry with my mom, but even more so with God. I pushed them both away. I became a slave to my flesh and a companion to fools.

The Lord instructs us to "Be sober, be vigilant; because your enemy, the devil, roams around incessantly, like a roaring lion looking for its prey to devour (1 Peter 5:8)." At this point in time, I wasn't sober; I was regularly using drugs and alcohol. I wasn't vigilant; I threw caution to the wind and put myself in many situations where I may not come out alive. I snuck out at night and attended parties with older men, frequently drove home drunk, and had unprotected sex. I even ran away from home and considered stripping to obtain money and affection from men.

The Lord also instructs us to "Enter through the narrow gate. For wide is the gate, and broad is the road that leads to destruction, and many enter through it. But small is the gate and narrow the road that leads to life, and only a few find it (Matthew 7:13-14)." I was headed towards destruction. My mom and grandparents did everything they possibly could to keep me on the right track, but the devil kept whispering lies in my ear. He convinced me that God had turned His back on me and abandoned me during my darkest hours.

Over the next several years, I continued to stumble my way through life without God. I was a ship attempting to navigate through the dark, raging sea without a moral compass or lighthouse of truth to help guide me. I allowed the devil to fill my head with more lies and my heart with an abundance of fear. I had a series of failed relationships; I clung to each new relationship so tight for fear of losing it that eventually, I did. My fear became a self-fulfilling prophecy.

My Grandma never gave up on me and continued to share God's Word and love with me. She would often write me letters that included scripture, devotions, and articles from various Christian publications. I would open each letter and instantly scoff and roll my eyes. Although my heart wasn't willing to hear or receive God's Word, the love I felt for my Grandma ran deep.

My world was shattered the day I received an unexpected call that Grandma had suffered a stroke after undergoing a "routine knee replacement surgery." I hung up and drove over an hour to the hospital. I wasn't prepared for what I saw; Her skin was pale and clammy, and her face was drooping and drooling on one side. She could barely speak or move. Her condition worsened over the next few months, and she started having seizures. Through it all, her faith never wavered, as she had built her house on the rock, which is Christ; She knew the troubles she faced were only temporary and that there was something better waiting for her in Heaven. During her final hours, she stated she was "in transition." She could hear the beautiful music playing in Heaven and the loved ones who had passed away speaking to her. The last thing she ever said to me was, "You are in my thoughts and prayers." My Grandpa was heartbroken after she passed, and his health quickly deteriorated. It wasn't long before he joined her in Heaven.

A day came when I was severely missing my grandparents, especially my Grandma. I was expecting a child, and my emotions were running high. I went downstairs and rummaged through several storage bins until I found what I was looking for – the letters from my Grandma. Although I barely glanced at them back when I first received them, now the words on their pages called to me and when I read them tasted like honey on my lips. I longed for my Grandma; however, I realized at that moment that what I longed for even more was her steadfast faith and a relationship with the Lord. I cried, and He heard me. I called on His name and instantly felt my heart soften, and His overwhelming love and presence filled the room. My grandma had never given up on me, and neither had He. He was there all along, patiently waiting for me to seek and trust Him with my whole heart and choose righteousness over sin.

I finally surrendered to God's Will, watered the mustard seed of faith that was planted in me by my Grandma, brought it into the light of God's Word, and have since continued to watch it bloom and grow. "Truly I tell you, if you have faith as small as a mustard seed, you can say to this mountain, 'Move from here to there,' and it will move. Nothing will be impossible for you (Matthew 17:20)."

Today my heart is no longer lukewarm but rather on fire for the Lord! He is continuing to refine me and turn my shame into glory. You don't need to be perfect to have a relationship with God. "Mercy triumphs over judgment (James 2:13)." Many of Jesus' disciples were far from perfect, and yet He still loved them, allowed them to learn from their mistakes, and used them to accomplish much in their lifetimes. The only person to live a sinless life was Jesus, and yet He willingly laid down His life to atone for the sins of all humanity. "God, who is rich in mercy, made us alive with Christ even when we were dead in transgressions – it is by grace you have been saved (Ephesians 2:4-5)."

God will continue to strategically move people in and out of my life to help fulfill His divine plan, and at times will allow the devil to tempt me and test my faith. I'll never again let the devil sift me as wheat or separate me from the love of God. "For I am convinced that neither death nor life, neither angels nor demons, neither the present nor the future, nor any powers, neither height nor depth, nor anything else in all creation, will be able to separate us from the love of God that is in Christ Jesus our Lord (Romans 8:38-39)."

There will be further spiritual battles; however, I'll fight them on my knees, wearing the full armor of God. I'll also have to sail through stormy seas; the Holy Spirit is now my compass and God's Word my lighthouse. I will not be blown and tossed by the wind!

I want everything I do now to bring glory to God and help others, like my Grandma, and to finish the work assigned to me by God – the work of telling others the Good News about the love and grace of God and the free gift of salvation through Jesus Christ. I want to meet the Lord face to face and have Him say to me, "Well done, good and faithful servant!"

If you can hold on, keep your thoughts on God and look to the future with hope, the Holy Spirit will help you withstand anything. "God works all things together for the good of those who love Him, who are called according to His purpose (Romans 8:28)." Come what may, the best is yet to come!

About - Melissa Magyar

Melissa Magyar currently lives with her family in charming and historic Stillwater, the birthplace of Minnesota. She is a devoted follower of Christ and child of the most high God, who has been blessed with a loving husband and three beautiful children.

Melissa works in aesthetic medicine as a Registered Nurse and Certified Laser Technician. She considers herself an artist and skincare humanitarian, helping restore youth and health back to aging and damaged complexions. Melissa took a huge leap of faith and opened her own Medical Spa, which continues to grow and flourish; it's won the local Readers' Choice Award for "Best Aesthetic Center" six years in a row.

Outside of work, she loves spending time with her family and French bulldog enjoying nature and activities such as biking, swimming, and gardening. Melissa has always been a skilled writer and is now using this gift to witness to others and glorify God. She is honored to be an author in the "I Cried, and He Heard Me" anthology. She hopes her struggles and intimate "Turning Shame Into Glory" testimony will help others.

One of Melissa's favorite Bible verses has become: "We can rejoice, too, when we run into problems and trials, for we know that they help us develop endurance. And endurance develops strength of character, and character strengthens our confident hope of salvation. And this hope will not lead to disappointment. For we know how dearly God loves us, because He has given us the Holy Spirit to fill our hearts with His love (Romans 5:3-5)."

Contact Info:
Email: melissamagyar81@gmail.com
Phone: 651-295-7695

I Was Done, But God Wasn't!
By Megan Fortner

My story begins in a home that didn't know Jesus and was full of yelling and abuse (mentally and physically). There was no love or stability. Can you resonate with that? My mom found love in the eyes of men, and she would deal with her emotions by drinking beer. When my mom would get drunk, she was mean. She would tell me I was stupid, wouldn't amount to anything, worthless, wished she never had me, and even went as far as to say, "I brought you in this world, and I'll take you out."

When I was five, she taught me how to play quarters, but in this game, I drank every time. My mom and her boyfriend thought that it was so funny. I got so sick. I remember my mom being so drunk that she wanted to get more beer, and she asked me to ride with her. On the way home, she passed out and almost ran off the side of the road with a big drop-off. I jumped up, put my foot on the brake, and slammed the car into park. I don't remember anything after that. There was a time my sister and I were so hungry that we had to sneak food into a Barbie bathtub. We hid it under the bed because we knew if she saw it, we would get a beating.

In my dad's home, there wasn't much love either. We had food, tons of toys, and land to play on, but there wasn't a lot of love or structure. We were only able to see him every other weekend. I remember when I threw a huge fit to stay with him. I wouldn't get out of the car, and when I did, I wouldn't let go of his leg. He spanked me so hard that my grandma came out of the house and got in his face. He just left. I remember thinking, why doesn't he want me? He knows what moms like. He knows that she drinks and beats us. I felt alone and abandoned. No one really wanted me. Then the day came when I got to live with my dad, and mom couldn't do anything about it. Mom left with a man for three days and left my older brother, myself, my two younger brothers, and two younger sisters at the house. I called my dad, and he picked us up. He took my older brother and me with him and the other siblings to my grandma. We took her to court, and she didn't show up. Dad won custody, and we were able to live with him. That was when I thought the beatings were going to stop.

When I got older, I jumped from house to house. I lived with my grandma and my dad most of the time. I started to hang out with boys and drink some. My dad would leave me home with my little sister a lot because he had to drive a truck to provide for us. It seems like I always had to be the parent. I had to get out. I found a love for sports, so I started to channel all my frustrations into them. I was at the highest point in my life when I played sports. I felt alive. I was in the papers every week and on leaderboards in our conference. Scouts were even coming to look at me. These were the best days of my life, I thought.

During my last year of high school, a youth pastor came in early in the mornings to minister to the children who attended. I went one morning, and something just hit my heart. What he was telling me I wanted. I wanted to know this, Jesus. I didn't want to live the way I was living anymore. I didn't want to find love in the eyes of boys. I didn't want to drink to fit in. I didn't want to be angry anymore. I decided I was going to give my life to Jesus. I know you hear that, and you believe everything changed right then, but it didn't. I confessed Jesus as my Lord, but there was no teaching, no leading, and no guiding. It seemed to me like the goal was to get as many people saved, and that was it—just a number on the saved list. I continued living my life trying to find Jesus and understand the Bible, but it wasn't working. Nothing was changing, so I gave up.

I got a scholarship to play basketball at an NAIA college. It was a Christian college, so I was excited to attend, thinking there wouldn't be a lot of drinking or drugs, and I would learn more about Jesus. I was wrong. There were drugs and alcohol everywhere. I went to a party one night with my basketball friends. I had one beer and woke up in a dorm room, completely naked, next to a man I didn't know. I got up, got dressed, and went to my dorm. That whole day I was replaying everything that happened that night in my head, trying to decide, did I do this? How did I get here? I went to the college nurse and asked for help. I had told her what had happened the night before. I told her that I felt like I had been slipped the date rape drug. Do you think that she listened to me? No! She said I went to a party, got drunk, and can't remember the rest. From that point, I started to spiral. I didn't attend my classes. I didn't do my homework. All I wanted to do was play basketball because I felt alive then. Finally, something in me broke, and I was done with college. This wasn't the life for me, so I decided to go home. When I went home, I fell right back into the way that I was when I was in high school.

I ended up getting pregnant with my daughter. There was nothing about that relationship that was good. There was abuse and manipulation. So much so that I felt like if I left, I wouldn't be able to keep my daughter. The grandmother had tried to make me believe that I needed to stay in the relationship because even though the father was never around, he choked me and mentally abused me, but he still loved me. Finally, I decided a month after Keylee was born enough was enough and got out of that relationship.

I met a man that I thought was my forever. He was nice, sweet, and caring. I thought I had hit the jackpot. After I had my son, I found out that he was cheating on me. That broke me more than anything because this was a man I thought loved me and treated me in a way I had never been treated before. I was broken, and I WAS DONE. What did this life have to offer me but hurt, sickness, depression, unworthiness, and disgust? I went outside and sat on the swing while my baby was in his crib, my daughter was at her dad's, and the thoughts were so strong. I sat there bawling and decided I would try this talking-to-God thing. I didn't know Him, but I heard He was there, so why not try talking to Him? I asked Him, "Why me? Why did no one want me? Why am I always used? How can people keep hurting me? I give everything that I have and get nothing but hurt? Nobody cares about me. I'm worthless. I'm never going to get out of this. Sound familiar? I decided I'd had enough. If I kill myself, then it'll be done. I won't have to deal with this anymore. I don't have to feel like this.

As I sat there trying to figure out which way I was going to do it and how my son would be found, an overwhelming feeling I've NEVER FELT BEFORE comes over me! Sitting right there on that swing at my weakest moment, I hear so loud, "You're not done because I'm not done with you. You are only just beginning. If you'll follow me and let everything else go. I will show you the way, and I will strengthen you beyond anything you could ever think or imagine. These negative thoughts are not yours. The devil wants you. Choose me and you will have the life I've had for you all along. Y'all, that changed my life!

I had a friend that was very strong in the Lord, so I reached out to her. I said I needed to go to church. She invited me, and I started going. I left my son's father, and that's when I found a man who truly loves God. We prayed together, and he looked at me in a way that I had never been looked at before. He didn't see me as a number on a headboard. He saw me for who God was creating me to be. We were engaged three months after we started dating and married two months later. We follow God together. We have amazing ministers who have grown us in the Word, Pastors Mark, and Trina Hankins. I wouldn't be where I am today without their leadership.

Since that day on the swing seven years ago, I've done, and I'm continually doing, exactly what God asked me to do faithfully. I think back to everyone who said I wouldn't amount to anything and that I would be just like my mother. I won't go anywhere in life, and I laugh. I have an amazing husband, we own our own business, and I am now an ordained minister. I travel all over the United States, ministering to people, children, abused, lost, sick, and poor. I have been on the radio now three times. I homeschool my two handsome, incredible, God-loving boys. I don't have to struggle with where my next meal is coming from, if our lights will be turned off, if I'll have a home, or if my husband will beat me or leave me.

I don't hurt anymore, and I'm not trying to get the approval of people. I am no longer a nobody, I'm a somebody, and I mean everything to God. There is nothing that will take me away from Him. Even if a storm, a trial, hardship, or people try to come against me, I know God has me on all sides. I'm not easily shaken. My feet are planted firmly on His Word. Oh yeah, I have people try to tell me about my past and still think of me as being that way. Do you know what I do? I laugh and say no, that person is dead and gone.

I'm a new creation in Christ Jesus. It is no longer I who lives but Christ who lives in me.

Now, I want to say this to you. Those negative thoughts and feelings are not yours. The devil wishes to have you, and if he can keep you depressed, sick, bound, and feeling worthless, then you will stay there. I'm here to tell you that GOD WILL do the same for you as He's done for me. Will it be easy? Not always because your flesh wants what the world has, but the real you, your spirit, wants what God has. God has a new life, healing, prosperity, love, goodness, strength, and boldness for you. The very purpose He created you for is still yours. You're not too late, never too old, to mess up, too broken to walk in ALL He has for you. All it takes is choosing Him and ALL He has for you.

Want everything He has for you and NOTHING LESS. Never settle for LESS than who God has created you to be. He has created you to be a warrior for yourself, your family, and all the others that are going to come behind you. You're made for GREATNESS. Walk in that GREATNESS. You have the same power as Christ in you. You are loved and wanted by the highest King in the whole universe. Even when everything and everyone is against you, He isn't, and He is the one who is going to see you through EVERYTHING. Some quotes that stick in my head that Pastor Mark says are, "You're not who your momma made you, you're not what your past made you, you're not what your circumstance made you, you're not who people say you are. You are exactly who God says you are. That's your TRUE IDENTITY". He also says, "Never let your struggle become your identity. Your identity is in Christ, and NO ONE takes that away from you but you!"

Jesus saved my life once and for all time on the cross, but He saved my life indefinitely on that swing, and HE WILL do the same for you if you let Him.

I want to take this moment to let you know you are not alone; I am here for you. I would love to stand with you, help you, and teach you how to stand against the devil, thoughts, and feelings. Connect with me on Facebook (Megan Fortner), Instagram, and by email: drivenwithapurpose@yahoo. We are in this together, and God is right in the middle of it. GOD LOVES YOU, and SO DO I! I Cried and He Heard Me!

About - Megan Fortner

Megan Fortner is a woman, on fire, after God's heart and plan for her life. Megan is very passionate about showing God's love and teaching others who they are and what they have in Christ.

Megan graduated ICIBC through Mark Hankins Ministers in February 2021. Since then, she has been traveling, bringing the Word over the radio and on social media! Anywhere God wants her to go or be, she is. Megan is currently working for Mark Hankins Ministries and loves it. There is no other place she wants to be!

Megan and her husband, Dustin, own their own outfitting business, Driven Purpose Outfitting, because it's all about the outdoors, hunting and God! They LOVE to hunt, and so do their boys. It's in their blood!

Megan is a coach at heart for the Kingdom of God and for basketball. She has been coaching 3rd-6th grade for six years. Teaching and leading are her passion. It's in her heart!

Currently in the works is a podcast, YouTube channel, and an app for her ministry. God's ways are higher than ours, and Megan is just honored to be the vessel!

Megan is a wife of an amazing husband and a momma to two amazing little boys, Ruger (8) and Kiaus (5). They all are currently living in Northern Missouri.

Contact Megan:
Drivenwithapurpose@yahoo.com
Facebook: Megan Fortner

Be Fierce, for You Are Destined!
By Dr. Deborah Allen

Destined - Developing as though according to a plan, certain to meet (a particular fate), intended for or traveling toward (a particular place).

Hear the clarion call to every warrior of God, for this anthology, is written and being birthed by fire through my very existence. As I pen and get this anthology ready to be published, I have lived through one of the greatest tests of my entire life. This path of my life has been fierce in this dispensation. Yet, "I cried, and he heard me!" Truly comprehend and recognize that we are destined. It has been predestined by the hand and mind of God that we would be born even made to be fierce! People of God, we are destined for greatness. Appreciate that fierceness resides in each of us.

We are destined by God for this fierce, royal battle called life. We have been orchestrated in the plan of our amazing God. Our life is our road map to our destiny. As I have aged, wisdom has been such a gift for me to truly see that our steps are ordered. God designed a purpose for each one of us. My existence is not a mistake but a blessing. God has always had me in his mind, even before the foundation of the world. I was not planned, but I am not a mishap. I was so destined to be here that God knows the very hairs on my head. I know the enemy has told us all our lives that we are a mistake. The enemy and even people have spoken that you are a waste of space. The devil has belittled and mocked us. However, that's all but a lie from the pit. We are destined, loved, chosen, wonderfully, and fearfully made. Even how we look, walk, talk, weigh, height, hair, and color; are all predestined. Our lives are so valuable that God mapped them out just for us. Our God took thought for our lives, planned for us, and set it all up for us to win. You are the apple of God's eye, and his favor rests upon us. We're so very loved. My existence, trials, hurts, setbacks, defeats, falls, disappointments, failures, stumbles, and victories are all in the plan of God. My life is written by the very hand of God. From being a preemie baby, molested as a child, teenage mother, suicidal wife, battered woman, divorcee, single, business owner, and Pastor, have all been destined and planned by God just for me.

How amazing that my life is not a surprise to God and our God knows how to perform all things well. Every experience of my life has been used to build, make, purify, mold, shape, and refine me. It all works according to God's vision. Rest assured that destiny has been in and at play in our lives. Our lives are not just thrown together as an afterthought. No, our lives are not chaotic messes. Destiny is before me and calls to me. "The steps of a good man are ordered by the LORD" (Ps. 37:23). My steps are ordered and mapped out clearly. God always planned for me to be victorious and be an overcomer. God destined me to win. We are born to win. Rest assured, you will accomplish the course of your life. God has a reason for us being alive. Our very fate is in the hand of our Savior. We can trust the all-knowing God with our lives. We belong to God and are his. The devil does not own us, but we are God's children. God is a faultless architect in this amazing and flawless plan of life.

Fierce--Having or displaying an intense or ferocious aggressiveness, violent in force, intensity. "And from the days of John the Baptist until now the kingdom of heaven suffereth violence, and the violent take it by force" (Matt. 11:12). Ding, ding, ding! That's the bell, and the battle has started for the people of God. Let's take up and fiercely fight against everything that is fighting us. Let's arm ourselves to rage war. Fiercely go to battle and subdue every Kingdom, salutation, or problem in your way. I mean utterly, destroy all the spiritual wickedness that's in high places. Let us be victorious and even snatch it by force. When I think of fierce, I think of tenacity, strength, endurance, and power. We must overcome all the attacks of the devil. Brawl, slash, kick, shed blood, struggle, and pursue victory.

Fierce makes me think of being in the military and having to defend ourselves at all costs. We are born gladiators. Gladiators can fight to the death against animals, even vicious attacks. Gladiators were made to be strong and invincible. They know to combat and truly fight for their lives. Remember, as the body of God, we are the defenders of the faith. Fierce is what God designed us to be. We are created in the image of a great, even terrible, God. We're designed and fashioned so we would last the test of time, trials, and tribulations. You are different (sanctified) from everyone else. God is a ferocious God, and he's breathed fierceness into us. Please watch the company we keep, for it determines our mindset. Our environment does play a part in our lives. Who we have fellowship with has a huge impact on us. Our association with other people has an influence on us.

Understand that we need to and must connect with strong people of purpose. We don't want to be connected to weak people or people who have no strength. Do not surround yourself with fearful or doubt-having folks. Fearful people will corrupt and pollute the entire camp. Scared people impute into our spirits stinking thinking and fearful words and thoughts. They speak only of defeat, even doubt. They just are plain old scared. They are already defeated in their own minds, and they can't even see the victory yet to come. We need people on our side, people that have our backs. I mean that it's important to build with that right tribe than when you are fighting, you know they are fighting too.

Through this passage of life, we must press forward and continue to war and fight the good fight of faith. "Fight the good fight of faith, lay hold on eternal life, whereunto thou art also called, and hast professed a good profession before many witnesses" 1 Tim. 6:12. We are witnesses to the fact that God is a deliverer. Our lives are a living testimony that is being seen and read by others. I have been through some trying times, yet those times caused me to "become" who God purposed me to be from the beginning. We've had to carry our crosses while walking with Christ.

"Behold, I give unto you power to tread on serpents and scorpions, and over all the power of the enemy: and nothing shall by any means hurt you." Luke 10:19. It took me a long time to understand this powerful truth. Glory to God! It made me fight, endure, go through, and win. It was always in my mind and heart to be great and be a world changer, but there was a time I struggled with this. About five years ago, I went through a stripping in my life that I thought was going to kill me! Remarkably the process allowed me to become her to be her. That meant I had to live through that time to become the best version of myself, and I reinvented myself. That season was a time of looking in my hand to see what I had to be great again. I had to do the hardest thing ever, and that was to get up again. Not only did I have to get up, but also I had to dream again. It was a season of purging, shifting, and self-growth. God rebuilt me to become better for the Kingdom and destiny. God is rebuilding you as well.

He is restoring you, and you will have a greater purpose and even stronger anointing upon your life. You are better equipped now to battle like never before. Not only that, God has made us better to focus and to lead. It's now your season and moment, so believe in yourself again. Glory to God; it's the time to reach for and acquire the blessings of the Lord. My God, my God, my God, is all I can say after that! All we must do is fight to win. Our families will be victorious. Our friends will be too. Yes, even our ministries will be elevated. Everything attached to us wins! We must be strong. We must stand God and be fierce!

The Fierce System:

F – Find yourself. Find your true self and be true to your own voice, dreams, and goals.

I – Indeed, be independent. Indeed be independent, for you are the difference maker in your life and the entire world.

E– Evaluate your life and story. Evaluate your story and life from clear eyes and not the eyes of your past and unlearned you.

R – Realize you make a difference. Realize life is better because you are here and have a purpose to fulfil.

C – Create opportunity through purpose. Create opportunity through purpose, the gift in your hand that will bring you before great men and allows you to make wealth.

E – Evolve into the greatest version of you. Evolve into the greatest version of you that the process of time has allowed you to become who you were born to be.

*** I have a free gift for you:
https://deborahallen.groovepages.com/free/index ***
SIGNATURE PROGRAM LINK
https://sites.google.com/view/executive-firce-coaching/home

About - Dr. Deborah Allen

Finding one's *inner voice* can be a liberating, awe-inspiring, and transformational experience. Fashioned to help the masses find their "fierce"; is the dynamic professional Deborah Allen.

Deborah Allen is a 22X best-selling & 11X international best-selling author, speaker, certified life coach, cleric, and C.E.O. and creative founder of **The Fierce System**, a multifaceted liaison specialty centered around helping women to both, find and develop their voice. Having been trained by world-renowned N.S.A. motivational speaker Mr. Les Brown, Deborah understands the importance of strategy, development, and credible mentorship, traits she seamlessly translates to her growing clientele.

Deborah's mantra is simple: Her one and only goal is to motivate clients, helping them to create the life they were meant to live.

Refusing mediocrity on all fronts, Deborah has trailblazed a credible path for those she serves. She has served as Senior Pastor of Lighthouse Apostolic Ministries of God Church for the last 23 years; and is the Executive Director of the nonprofit organization L.A.M. Ministries, Inc.

Matching servant leadership with incredible respect for higher learning, Deborah is a Certified Life Coach; and is a member of the National Speaker Association Speaker (N.S.A.) and a Black Speakers Network (B.S.N.) Speaker. Her conglomerate, The Fierce System, is comprised of many platforms, including Fierce T.V., Radio, and blog; as well as Fierce Voices of Destiny Program; where she mentors, develops and creates strategic alignment between clients and their true life's calling. She is the Visionary and C.E.O. of Igniting The Flame Publishing, Visionary Coaching & Consulting Group L.L.C., and Deborah Allen Enterprise.

Deborah proudly attests that women are at the heartbeat of all she does and that it is her desire to see them be strong and fierce and know that they can truly achieve their dreams and walk in purpose. When she is not out helping women to come alive, rebuild, shift and find themselves again, Deborah is a valued asset to her communal body and a loving member of her family and friendship circles.

Dr. Deborah Allen. Energizer. Organizer. Servant Leader.
Contact Information: Apostle/Ambassador Dr. Deborah Allen
www.deborahallenfierce.com
www.ignitingtheflamepublishing.com
Email: deborahallenfierce@gmail.com

Links:
Facebook: https://www.facebook.com/deborahalle nfierce
Instagram: https://www.instagram.com/deborahallenfi erce/
Twitter: https://twitter.com/deborahallenfie
YouTube: https://www.youtube.com/channel/UCTOf0i gcAxlVaneH2ZOo_Zg
2nd Website: https://deborahallenspeaker.com/

Made in USA - North Chelmsford, MA
1353586_9798372311732
02.07.2023 1814